Men Around the Messenger

COMPANIONS OF THE PROPHET ﷺ SERIES

PART II

Men Around the Messenger

COMPANIONS OF THE PROPHET ﷺ SERIES

PART II

Khalid Muhammed Khalid

1 2 3 4 5 6 7 8 9 10

Khalid Muhammed Khalid

Men around the Messenger

Part II

ISBN 978-1-915570-07-9

www.lightpublishing.co.uk

بسم الله الرحمن الرحيم

CONTENTS

INTRODUCTION

History recognises the great company of men that first followed in the footsteps of the Prophet Muhammad ﷺ. During the age of the Companions, all records required extraordinary attention to detail. And so, we are now left with a plethora of well-researched documentation about that period of Islamic history, and about the men around the Prophet ﷺ.

Successive generations of scholars have subjected even the smallest details of their lives to a great deal of scrutiny. These men's lives are not stuff of legend. These are facts characteristic of the personalities of the Prophet's own Companions. They are exalted and ennobled, not because of the author of their stories, but because of what the Companions themselves desired, and the immense effort they made to attain perfection.

They devoted their entire lives to the cause of Islam, offering personal sacrifice in their dedication to the Messenger ﷺ and to his call to faith. When the world was craving for someone to remove the shackles from a troubled humanity, these Companions stood by their great Messenger as pioneers.

One can only imagine how those righteous men achieved what they did in just a few years. How did they triumph over the ancient world, with all its empires and sovereignties? How did they build a new world with Allah's Quran and His Words? Above all, how were they able to illuminate human conscience with the truth of monotheism, forever sweeping away centuries of ancient paganism? This was their real miracle.

Of course, their achievements were simply a modest reflection of the greater miracle that was, and is, Allah's noble Quran. On the day that His honourable Messenger was commanded to deliver the message, Islam began to offer enlightenment to all.

In this book, we present 60 personalities of the Prophet's Companions, (may Allah have mercy upon them all). As mentioned at the conclusion of this book, these 60 men represent several thousand others of their brethren, who were contemporaneous with the Messenger ﷺ, and who also believed in and supported him. In their reflection we see the images of all the Companions. We recognise their faith, their constancy, their heroism and their loyalty to Allah and His Messenger ﷺ. And we will see here the effort they exerted, the calamities they endured, and the victory they achieved.

Now, let us discover more about these righteous men, to better understand the most graceful and virtuous of human examples. Let us see under their humble outer appearances, and discover the most sublime of people in greatness and wisdom. Let us appreciate their piety, and follow their stories as they spread the faith of Islam to liberate mankind.

Khalid Muhammad Khalid

MUHAMMAD ﷺ THE LIGHT THEY FOLLOWED

Muhammad ibn Abdullah became Allah's Messenger ﷺ in the midsummer of his life. He was always filled with greatness and honesty, modesty and loyalty. He was devoted to the truth, and revered both life and the living. Allah's bounty towards him was great. He bestowed upon him the blessing of carrying His standard and speaking on His behalf.

It was Muhammad's rare eminence that secured his Companions' loyalty and made him a teacher and a friend to them. Companions such as Abu Bakr, Talhah, Az-Zubair, Uthman ibn Affan, Abdur Rahman ibn Awf, and Sa'ad ibn Abu Waqqas, *all* abandoned their wealth and glory in favour of Islam. With that choice came heavy burdens in life, and a great deal of conflict. But, still more hastened to his call.

What made those who believed in the Prophet ﷺ only increase in number? Though he declared day and night, "I hold no good or harm for you. I do not know what will become of me or you!" What then made them believe that the Quran they were reciting in secret, would one day reverberate in strong tones - not only in their own society, but throughout the ages, the world over? What made them believe the prophecy brought to them by the Messenger ﷺ? What filled their hearts with certainty and perseverance?

Of course, it was Muhammad ibn Abdullah himself.

They saw with their own eyes all his virtues and all that distinguished him. They saw his chastity, his purity, his honesty, his straightforwardness and his courage. They saw his eloquence and witnessed, first-hand, his daily revelations. These men watched Muhammad grow up and were his contemporaries throughout his life. His childhood was not limited to close relations, but instead witnessed by the people of Makkah as a whole. That was because his childhood was not like any other, it drew attention to itself for its early signs of maturity.

For example, the Quraysh used to talk about Abdul Muttalib's grandson who kept away from the children's playgrounds. And whenever he was invited to their celebrations, he would say, "I was not created for that." When his wet nurse, Halima, took him back to his people, she too told them about her observations, her experience with the child and what she saw in him to convince them that he was no ordinary boy. She believed there was a hidden secret in him, unknown except to Allah, which might be revealed one day.

And so it was that Muhammad ﷺ had a transparent life, from cradle to grave. His every step, every word, every movement, every dream were the right of all people from the day he was born. It was as if Almighty Allah wished to highlight his reason and intellect through the transparency of his deeds.

If throughout a person's life you have only known them to be pure, truthful and honest, is it logical that such a person would suddenly start telling lies after the age of 40? Would he lie about Allah in order to claim he was His Messenger ﷺ, chosen and inspired by Him? Intuitively, no. This was the attitude of, not only the early believers, but also the Muhajirun (Emigrants) towards Allah's Messenger ﷺ, and indeed all those who sheltered him. They saw him not only sharing the trouble and hunger that befell people, but establishing for himself a core principle which was, "To be the first to feel hunger if people go hungry, and the last to satisfy [one's] hunger when people [are] starving." A man who had such an enlightened life could not play false with Allah. So, the believers saw the light of Allah, and they too began to follow Him.

Many unperceived blessings and spoils were bestowed upon the Companions, while the Prophet himself became more modest, more austere and more pious. Throughout his life, it was clear that such a man was not seeking wealth, money or sovereignty. When these were offered to him in recognition of his triumphant leadership, Muhammad ﷺ rejected them all. Till his last breath he devoted himself only to Allah - repentant and chaste.

He never deviated from the purpose of his great life, and never broke a promise to Allah in worship. No sooner would the latter part of the night begin, than he would get up, make his ablution and invoke Allah's name. Mountains of wealth and money were accumulated on his behalf, yet he never took more from it than the poorest of the Muslims would. He died leaving only his armour to bequeath.

Kings and countries received his invite to Islam with awe. But, not an atom of arrogance befell his character. When he saw people approaching him in nervous reverence, he said to them "Be easy, my mother used to eat dried meat in Makkah." Such was his humility.

When he conquered Makkah, the enemies of his faith put down their weapons and bowed their heads to await his judgment. But, he merely said, "Disperse, you are free!" Even at the height of the victory (to which he had devoted his life), he deprived himself of it. Instead, he walked in the victory procession on the Day of the Conquest with his head bowed. He repeated prayers of thanks to Allah in low tones, eyes wet with tears until he reached the Kaba. He then confronted the idols and said, "*Truth has come and falsehood has vanished, indeed, falsehood is bound to vanish.*" (17:81)

He was a man who spent his young life in purity and contemplation. After he received the revelation, he spent the remainder of his days in worship, guidance, and struggle. How could such a man be a liar? Surely, such a man and such a Messenger was above that. His Companions agreed.

We have mentioned that logic and reason were - and still are - the best proof of the truth for Muhammad ﷺ when he said, "I am Allah's Messenger." It does not appeal to good logic or to sound reason that a man who lived such a good life would lie about Allah. Early believers who hastened to believe in his message, and whom we are honoured to know something about through the pages of this book, believed in such logic. We see Muhammad ﷺ before his message and we see him after his message. We see him in his cradle and we see him near the grave. But, have we seen any contradiction or inconsistency in his life? Never.

Let us now approach the first years of his message. Those were the years that opened the living book of his life and heroism and, more than any other years, represented the cradle of his miracles. Throughout those years, the Messenger of Allah ﷺ was alone. He left all the possessions of comfortable, secure and settled life. He approached the people with what they were not familiar with, or rather with what they detested. He approached them and chose his words to appeal their reason, rather than emotions. It was a difficult task indeed, and so he approached it with an artfulness specific to him.

During Muhammad's time people worshipped idols, and their rites were observed as a religion. The Messenger ﷺ did not use the path of least resistance. It would have been easier for him to avoid direct confrontation, but he chose not to. This illustrates that he was indeed a Messenger. He heard a divine voice within him telling him to rise, and he did so willingly. He confronted his people in the plainest of terms, saying: "O people, I am the Messenger of Allah unto you, to worship Him and not to set partners with Him. These idols are intellectual falsehood. They are of no harm or benefit to you."

One might think that after this initial show of dedication, Muhammad ﷺ would worship his Lord as he liked, generally leaving the deities and his community's religion alone. If such a notion occurred to some Makkans at that time, the Prophet soon dispelled it. He made it quite clear that as a Messenger, he had a message to convey, and that he would not stay silent after receiving such guidance. In fact, nothing could have silenced him, because it was Allah who caused him to speak, and guided his footsteps.

The Quraysh's response was swift. One day, the noblemen of the Quraysh complained to Abu Talib: "Verily, we cannot tolerate a person who insults our fathers, mocks our dreams and finds fault with our deities. You either stop him, or we fight both of you until one of the parties is destroyed." Abu Talib sent a message to his nephew saying, "My nephew, your people have approached me and talked about your affairs. You have to think of me and yourself and not burden me with what I cannot endure."

The Messenger ﷺ did not hesitate and was resolute in his response: "O uncle, by Allah, if they put the sun on my right and the moon on my left in order to abandon this matter until it is manifested by Allah or I perish by it, I would never abandon it." Abu Talib thereupon restored his courage and the courage of his forefathers at once, clasped the right hand of his nephew with his two hands, and said, "Say what you like, for, by Allah, I will never force you to do anything at all."

From this point onwards, Muhammad ﷺ did not depend on his uncle for protection (though his uncle was capable of that) but he himself bestowed security, protection and steadfastness on the people around him. This inspired their love, loyalty, and belief in the Messenger ﷺ.

His persistence regarding truth, his perseverance with the message and his patience during great troubles were all for the sake of Allah and not for any personal benefit. Such sacrifices were bound to attract the attention of brilliant minds, and those with good conscience. His Companions watched as harm reached the Prophet ﷺ from every corner. The solace he had sought in his uncle Abu Talib and his wife Khadija was also soon denied to him because they both died within days of each other.

The persecution became incredibly intense after this. One day for instance, the Messenger ﷺ went to the Kaba where the nobles of the Quraysh laid in wait for him as he performed his circumambulation. Suddenly, they surrounded him saying, "Is it you that says (such-and-such a thing) about our deities?" He calmly answered them "Yes, I say that." They held him by the ends of his clothes while Abu Bakr pleaded with them for his release: "Are you going to kill a man for saying, Allah is my Lord?"

As if the hostility from his own clan wasn't enough, the Prophet ﷺ was subjected to further abuse from those who were not related or known to him. But, Almighty Allah had commanded him to deliver the message, and so he did not falter. He would often remember a time when the intransigence of his community was so intense, that he returned home sorrowful, and huddled to cover himself in his bed. In that moment he heard the voice of revelation urging him to rise once more: *O You covered - Arise and warn.* (74:1-2)

So, he persisted in delivering Allah's message and warning against deviation. He did not care about harm befalling him, and he did not search for comfort. When he visited Taif to spread his message, the nobles of the community there were more cunning than their Makkan counterparts. Instead of abusing him themselves, they set their children and hooligans against him - abandoning the most sacred custom of the Arabs, that of hospitality to guests and the protection of one who seeks help.

Muhammad ﷺ escaped to a nearby orchard during the pursuit of the hooligans. His right hand was stretched towards heaven praying to Allah while his left protected his face from the stones being thrown at him. Even in such a stressful moment, the Prophet called to his Creator with courtesy and eloquence: "O Allah, to you I complain of the weakness of my strength, my inability to find a way, and my humiliation by the people. O the Most Compassionate, You are the Lord of the weak, and You are my Lord. To whom do You entrust me? To a distant relation who ignores me, or to an enemy who has power over me? If you are not angry with me, I do not care for other things, but granting me your mercy is too generous of you. I seek refuge in the light of Your face that brightens the darkness and amends the affairs of this world and the next. Do not be angry or dissatisfied with me. I beg your favour until You are satisfied with me. There is no strength or power except through You."

What loyalty the Prophet ﷺ had to his call to Islam! He was an unarmed person facing plots at every turn, and yet he persisted, staying steadfast to Allah. On his return from Taif, the Makkan people did not sense any despair in him. In fact, he became more optimistic and more dedicated. He decided to present himself to other local tribes, reaching out to them in their own districts. One day he went to Banu Kindah, another day Banu Hanifah, then to Banu Amir and so on, from one tribe to another. He said to them all, "I am the Messenger of Allah to you. He commands you to worship Allah and not to take partners with him, and to abandon what you worship of idols." When he visited nearby tribes, Abu Lahab would follow him and say to the people, "Do not believe him, for he is calling you to what is false."

People watched on as the Messenger of Allah sought other believers and helpers, but he was met only with ingratitude and enmity. He also refused any bargains and worldly gains in exchange for faith, and so he continued to struggle.

People marvelled at Muhammad ﷺ, but few believed in him. Despite their low numbers, his fellow Muslims provided him with comfort and company. But then the Quraysh decided that each tribe should be in charge of teaching the believers amongst them a lesson. So, suddenly, a storm of persecution descended upon the Muslims. It was at this point that Muhammad ﷺ surprised the community by ordering all Muslims to emigrate to Abyssinia to seek sanctuary with the Christian king there.

The Prophet, however, decided to remain in Makkah to face the Quraysh's aggression. Why not emigrate with them and convey the word of Allah in another place? After all, Allah is the Lord of the worlds, not the Lord of the Quraysh alone. Furthermore, there were among the Muslims a good number of the noblest families of the Quraysh. Some of the most powerful tribes represented were Banu Umaiyah (Uthman ibn Affan, Amr ibn Sa'id ibn Al-As and Khalid ibn Sa'id ibn Al-As), Banu Asad (Az-Zubair ibn Al-Awam, Al-Aswad ibn Nawfal, Yazid ibn Zamah, and Amr ibn Umaiyah), and finally Banu Zahrah (Abdur Rahman ibn Awf, Amir ibn Abu Waqqas, Malik ibn Ahyab, and Al-Muttalib ibn Azhar). Many of the families of these Muslims would not stand their relatives' persecution for much longer. Why, then, did the Messenger ﷺ not let them stay with him to support him and to show his power?

Of course, he did not want a civil war, even if the probability of success weighed in his favour. But it was the Messenger's compassion above all that drove this decision. He could not bear to see his people being persecuted unnecessarily because of him. Of course, sacrifice could be made where there was no other choice, but when suffering was avoidable, it only made sense to send the Muslims to safety. But again, why not join them too? Simply, he was not commanded to. His place was to remain among the idols, to keep uttering Allah's name in their midst. He continued to be harmed for his beliefs, but he stayed steadfast and held true to his sacrifice.

The man and the Messenger manifested perfectly in Muhammad ﷺ. Those who doubted his message had no such doubts about his reputation, the purity of his character, or his humanity. Allah had chosen a man who was the best in both standing and honesty. The Prophet was heard reprimanding others if they ever exaggerated in glorifying him, or even sometimes when they simply over complimented him. If they were seated when he walked in a room, he prohibited them from standing up to honour him. He said, "Do not stand as non-Arabs do when they glorify one another."

When the sun eclipsed on the day of the death of his beloved son Ibrahim, the Muslims mentioned that the eclipse must have been a reflection of sadness for the loss of his son. But even in his state of mourning, the Messenger ﷺ hastened to refute this assumption before it became legend. He addressed them saying, "The sun and the moon are two of the signs of Allah. They never eclipse for the death or life of anybody."

Muhammad ﷺ was entrusted with the minds of his people, and so accomplishing his task and spreading Islam in the right way was crucial to him. He was certain that he came to humanity to change their way of life and that he was not a Messenger to the Quraysh, or even to the Arabs alone; but he was Allah's Messenger to all people on earth.

Almighty Allah directed his vision and the Prophet ﷺ perceived the truth of the faith he announced and the living immortality it would have. Nevertheless, he did not see himself or his unprecedented success as more than a brick in the construction. As he once said, "The relation between prophets who came before me and myself is like a man who built a house and constructed it well and decorated it, except for a brick in one of its corners. This made people go round it and express their astonishment, saying, will this brick not be put in place? I am such a brick and I am the last of the prophets."

All that long life he lived - all his struggles and heroism, his glory and purity, all the victory achieved after his death - all of this was nothing but a brick, a mere brick in a lofty and deep-rooted building. He was the one who proclaimed this and reiterated it. In addition, he did not make up such a speech out of assumed modesty, or to nourish a hunger for glory. He emphasised this brick analogy because it was fact and quintessential to his message.

That was the teacher of mankind and the last of the prophets. He was the light seen by the people, and he lived amongst them just as any other man. Then, after his departure from this world, he was seen by the whole world as a preserver of truth.

Now, while we meet a number of his noble Companions on the following pages of this book - where we will be astonished by their faith, their sacrifices, and the good cause they set their lives for – the reason for their marvellous lives will be clear before us.

This reason was nothing but the light they followed in Muhammad, the Messenger of Allah ﷺ. Almighty Allah combined in him the vision of truth and self-dignity, which illuminated the destiny of mankind.

(24)

UMAIR IBN WAHB

From 'Satan of the Quraysh' to A Disciple of Islam

On the Day of Badr, Umair was one of the leaders who took up weapons to put an end to Islam. He was sharp-sighted and a perfect estimator, so his people delegated him to determine the number of Muslims who came forth with the Messenger. He was also tasked with checking if the Muslims had ambushers or reinforcements behind them. Umair ibn Wahb Al-Jamli galloped on his horse round the camp of the Muslims, then returned to his people and told them that there were about 300 men - and his estimation was right.

They asked him if they had reinforcements behind them. He said, "I found nothing. But O you Quraysh, I saw horses carrying veritable death. They have neither fortitude nor refuge except their swords. By Allah, I see if one of them is killed, one of you will be killed also. If they killed the same number as you, what would be the benefit of life after that? Think wisely."

Some of the leaders of the Quraysh were affected by his words and were about to gather their men to return to Makkah without fighting. However, Abu Jahl swayed their opinion and reignited the spiteful fire of war, in which he was ironically the first victim.

The Quraysh gave Umair the epithet 'The Satan of Quraysh'. On the Day of Badr, he fought fiercely and wildly, but the forces of the Quraysh returned to Makkah completely beaten. Umair ibn Wahb even left a part of himself in Medina, as the Muslims took his son as a prisoner of war. One day, he joined his cousin Safwan ibn Umaiyah who was chewing on the thought of his enemies with great bitterness. Safwan's father Umaiyah ibn Khalaf had been killed at Badr and his bones buried at Al-Qalib. So, Safwan and Umair sat together ruminating on their enemies. Urwah ibn Az-Zubair's following account retells their conversation:

Mentioning those who were killed at Badr, Safwan said, "By Allah, there isn't any good in life after them." Umair said, "That's true. By Allah, were it not for debts that I'm unable to repay and my children who I fear might be vagabonds after me, I would ride to Muhammad and kill him. I have a plausible reason to give him. I'll say that I have come for the sake of my son, a prisoner of war."

Safwan seized the chance and said, "I'll repay your debts and maintain your children with mine and comfort them as long as they live." Umair agreed and said, "Keep it secret." Then he ordered his sword to be sharpened and poisoned, and set out.

When he arrived at Medina, Umar ibn Al-Khattab was sitting among some of the Muslims talking about the Day of Badr. Umar looked and saw Umair ibn Wahb, girded with his sword, making his camel kneel at the door of the mosque. Umar said, "That dog, the enemy of Allah, Umair ibn Wahb! By Allah, he has come for nothing but evil. It is he who provoked us on the Day of Badr."

Umar entered and said to the Messenger ﷺ, "O Prophet of Allah, here is the enemy of Allah, Umair ibn Wahb come girded with his sword." The Prophet said, "Let him in." Umar came and took him by the scabbard of his sword round his neck and said to some of the Muslims around him, "Enter and sit with the Prophet ﷺ and be cautious of that fellow, he is dishonest." Then Umar entered, still holding Umair by the scabbard of the sword. When the Prophet saw him, he told Umar to let him alone and said to Umair, "Draw nearer."

Umair approached and said, "Good morning." That was the salutation from the period of jahiliyya. The Prophet ﷺ said, "Allah has honoured us with a better salutation than yours. It is As-Salam, the salutation of the believers in Paradise." Umair said, "O, Muhammad, by Allah I have heard it recently." The Prophet said, "What made you come, Umair?" Umair said, "I have come for the sake of this captive in your hands." The Prophet said, "Tell the truth, Umair, what have you come for?" Umair, "I have come for that purpose." The Prophet ﷺ said, "But you sat with Safwan ibn Umaiyah at Al-Hijr and mentioned those of Al-Qalib from the Quraysh, then you said, were it not for my debts and my children, I would ride and kill Muhammad. Safwan promised to repay your debts and maintain your children on condition that you kill me, but Allah prevented you from doing so."

At the moment, Umair burst into tears. He proclaimed, "I witness that there is no god but Allah and that you are His Prophet. That matter wasn't attended by anyone except Safwan and me. By Allah, Allah told it to you. Praise be to Allah who guided me to Islam." The Prophet ﷺ said to his Companions, "Teach your brother the religion and how to reach the Quran and set free the prisoner of war."

Thus, Umair ibn Wahb unexpectedly embraced Islam. The former 'Satan of the Quraysh' was so overwhelmed by the light of the Prophet ﷺ and Islam that, in a moment, he embraced the faith and became known henceforth as the 'Disciple of Islam'. Umar ibn Al-Khattab, (may Allah be pleased with him) once said, "By Allah, I hated him more than I hated a pig, when he appeared. But now, I love him more than I love some of my sons."

Umair sat thinking deeply about the tolerance of this religion and the greatness of its Prophet. He remembered his previous days in Makkah when he was arguing and fighting against Islam before the hijra of the Prophet ﷺ and his Companions to Medina. Then he remembered his fighting on the Day of Badr and his coming on this day to kill the Prophet. All that was abolished, the moment he said, "There is no god but Allah, and Muhammad is His Messenger."

What tolerance! What purity and self-confidence this great religion carries. Muslims forgave all his crimes and hate, opened their hearts and embraced him. In that moment, Umair became one of the Muslims and one of the Prophet's own Companions, with the rights and duties that entailed. Did not he, whom Umar ibn Al-Khattab wanted to kill a short time ago, become dearer to Umar than his own sons? Such is the glory and splendour of Islam.

Within a short period of time, Umair knew that his duty towards this religion was to serve it as much as he had fought it. To support it as much as he had conspired against it, and to show Allah and His Prophet what they liked of truth, struggle, and obedience.

Thus, soon after his conversion he came to the Prophet and said "O Prophet of Allah, I had been doing my best to put out the light of Allah and was fond of hurting the Muslims. I would like you to give me permission to go to Makkah to call them to Allah, His Prophet and to Islam. Allah may guide them, otherwise, I'll hurt them in their religion as I used to hurt your companions in their religion."

From the time Umair left Makkah for Medina, Safwan ibn Umaiyah (who had persuaded Umair to go and kill the Messenger) walked proudly in the streets of Makkah. His people asked him how he could be so merry, when the bones of his father were still warm in the sands of Badr. Safwan proudly rubbed his hands together and said to the people, "After a few days, happy news will come and make you forget the Battle of Badr." Every morning he went out of Makkah and asked the caravans, "Hasn't any matter occurred in Medina?" Their answers were in the negative, as none of them had seen or heard of any unusual event.

Safwan continued asking caravan after caravan, until one day he met one and said to them, "Hasn't anything taken place in Medina?" The traveller said, "Yes, a very important matter occurred." With a radiant face Safwan asked the traveller, "What happened? Tell me!" The man said, Umair ibn Wahb has embraced Islam, and he is there learning the religion and the Quran!" Safwan felt light-headed. The good news promised to his people to make them forget the Battle of Badr was dreadful enough to cause his ruin.

One day, Umair returned to Makkah holding his sword, ready to fight, and Safwan ibn Umaiyah was the first who met him. No sooner did Safwan see Umair, than he got ready to attack him, but the combat-ready sword in Umair's hand dissuaded him. Safwan was satisfied with flinging some insults at Umair, then went on his way.

Umair re-entered Makkah as a Muslim and saw his home through eyes anew. He recalled Umar ibn Al-Khattab's words upon Umair's embracing of Islam, and cried, "By Allah! I'll sit as a believer in every place I sat as a polytheist." Taking these words as his motto, Umair made up his mind to sacrifice his life for the religion that he had once fought boldly against. And thus, he began to compensate for what he had missed and to race with time by calling to Islam day and night, both secretly and openly.

In his heart, faith flooded upon him with safety, guidance, and light. On his tongue were words of truth, calling others to justice, charity, and good. Within a few weeks, countless numbers embraced Islam under the guidance of Umair ibn Wahb. Umair set forth with them to Medina in a delightfully long caravan.

On the day of the Conquest of Makkah, Umair did not forget to call his companion and relative, Safwan, to Islam. Particularly as there was no doubt in the truth of the Prophet ﷺ and his mission. Safwan had travelled to Jeddah on his way to Yemen by sea. Umair pitied him so much that he decided to do all he could to help him. He hurried to the Prophet ﷺ and said, "O Prophet of Allah, Safwan ibn Umaiyah is the chief of his people. He set off escaping from you to throw himself into the sea. Give him safety. Peace be upon you." The Prophet said, "He is safe." Umair said "O Prophet of Allah, give me a token for his safety." The Prophet gave him his turban which he had worn when he entered Makkah.

Urwah ibn Az-Zubair narrated the story as follows. He relates that Umair set off till he reached Safwan when he was about to sail. Umair said, "O Safwan, I sacrifice my mother and father for you. Avert perishing yourself. This is the safety of the Prophet of Allah ﷺ I came to you with." Safwan said to him, "Woe to you! Go away, don't speak to me." Umair said to him, "O Safwan! I sacrifice my mother and father for you. The Prophet of Allah is the best, the most righteous, and the most clement of all people. His glory is yours and his honour is yours." Safwan said, "I'm afraid." Umair said, "He's more clement and more generous than that."

Umair returned with him until they came to the Prophet ﷺ. Safwan said to the Prophet, "He claims that you have given me safety." The Prophet said, "He speaks the truth. Safwan said to the Prophet, "Give me the option for two months." The Prophet ﷺ said, "You have the option for four months." After a while Safwan embraced Islam, and Umair was extremely happy about his acceptance of Islam.

And in this way, Ibn Wahb continued on in his blessed journey to Allah by following the great Prophet ﷺ. And it was through the Prophet Muhammad that Allah saved people such as Umair - by taking them out of the depths of darkness, into the light.

(25)

ABU AD-DARDA

A Wise Man's Remembrance of Allah

While the armies of Islam were advancing on victoriously, there lived in Medina a wonderful philosopher and wise man whose wisdom advanced Islam through the power of his words. He would often say, "Can I tell you about the best of your deeds which are more thriving and better than invading your enemies, cutting their throats and cutting yours, and better than dirhams and dinars?" Those who listened eagerly asked, "And what is that, O Abu Ad-Darda?" Abu Ad-Darda's face glittered with the light of faith and wisdom and said, "The remembrance of Allah; the remembrance of Allah is the greatest thing in life."

That wonderful man did not preach an isolationist philosophy. He was not preaching negativism, nor was he recommending any retreat from the responsibilities of a new religion. But, Abu Ad-Darda found true solace in contemplation, and he dedicated his life to seeking truth. He was the wise man of those days (may Allah be pleased with him) and he believed that Islam, with all its duties, was indeed the only ideal way to truth.

Thus, he was engrossed by his faith, dedicating himself to it and moulding his life accordingly. He was an embodiment of this Quranic verse (that he oft-repeated): *Truly, my prayer and my devotion, my life and my death are all for Allah, the Lord of the Worlds.* (6:162) Abu Ad-Darda achieved a high state of spirituality, and personally dedicated his life to Allah, the Cherisher of the Worlds.

Now, let us imagine approaching this wise man. Do you observe the light that radiates from his forehead? Do you smell the good perfume coming from his direction? It is the light of wisdom and the perfume of faith. His mother was asked about what he liked best; she answered, "Contemplation and consideration." He would often urge his companions to contemplate, by saying to them, "Contemplation for an hour is better than worshipping for the whole night."

On the day he embraced Islam and pledged his allegiance to the Prophet ﷺ as a Muslim, he was a successful trader of Medina. Only a short time after he accepted Islam, he decided to change his habits altogether. He himself explained: "I embraced Islam at the hands of the Prophet ﷺ and I was a trader. I wanted to combine trade and worship, but they would never go together. I abandoned trade and retained worship. Today, it doesn't please me to sell and buy to earn 300 dinars a day, although my shop is at the door of the mosque. I can't say that Allah forbids selling, but I'd like to be of those whom neither traffic nor merchandise can divert from remembrance of Allah."

In spite of his success as a trader, he was a man searching for spiritual excellence and perfection of character. He wanted his worship to create a ladder between him and Allah, so that he could attain true goodness. If he wanted worship to be merely another duty, he would have been able to manage both his worship and his trade. Of course, there are many good and pious people working in trade. Among the Companions of the Prophet of Allah ﷺ, there were those men whom "neither traffic nor merchandise could divert from the remembrance of Allah". But they worked hard to develop their trade, by which they satisfied the needs of the Muslims and actually served the cause of Islam. Each Companion had his own path in life, and neither one's life choices diminished the other.

Abu Ad-Darda simply felt that he was created for seeking the truth. He secluded himself from daily life till he burnished and sanctified his soul. This made Abu Ad-Darda into a great teacher and an upright, wise man. Many a happy student came to listen to him. He was influenced to the core of his being by the saying of Prophet: "Little and satisfied is better than much and diverted." And Allah Almighty's words: *Woe to every taunting slanderer, backbiter, who piles up wealth and counts over it again and again, thinking that his wealth will make him immortal!* (104:1-3)

The Messenger of Allah ﷺ also said, "Leave the worries of life as far as possible," and "He who makes life his only aim, Allah will sunder his unity and make poverty between his two eyes. He who makes the Hereafter his only goal, Allah makes riches in his heart and makes every good hurry to him." Therefore, Abu Ad-Darda lamented over those who fell captive to the ambition of wealth and said, "I seek refuge with the Lord from the dispersion of the heart." He was asked, "What is dispersion of the heart, Abu Ad-Darda?" He answered, "That means I have money everywhere." He called people to truly possess life, by doing without it. Then he said, "He who cannot do without life, is lifeless."

According to his opinion, money should only be a means to a content life. Thus, people should take it legitimately (in a halal way) and earn it kindly, not by coveting it greedily. He said, "Don't eat anything unless it is good, don't earn any money unless it is good, don't take anything to your house unless it is good." He also wrote to his companions saying, "After that, any temporary thing you possess in life was possessed by someone else before you, and will be owned by another after you, and you have nothing except what you offered to yourself."

He also advised on the merits of inheritance when he advised: "Give preference over yourself to him from whom you are collecting money for your sons to inherit, since you collect money for one of the two: either a good son who spends the money in obedience to Allah, thus he will be happy with what you earned and free from troubles; or a disobedient son who spends it in sins and disobedience to Allah, and so you will be tortured by what you had collected for him. Entrust their living to the Bounty of Allah and save yourself."

Abu Ad-Darda's view of life itself was that it is merely ours on loan. When Cyprus was conquered and the booty carried to Medina, people saw Abu Ad-Darda visibly weeping. Astonished, they approached and Jubair ibn Nufair said to him, "Why are you weeping on the day that Allah supported Islam and the Muslims?" Abu Ad-Darda replied wisely, "Woe to you, Jubair! What trifling things creatures are, if they leave the commands of Allah. It was the best nation, having dominion, but it left the commands of Allah, and therefore it came to what you see." He reasoned that the quick collapse of Cyprus to the armies of Islam was caused by a spiritual bankruptcy. So, he feared a similar outcome for the Muslims in the near future, when the ties of faith would decline and the bonds to Allah, truth, and goodness would weaken. Consequently, the loan would be taken from their hands as easily as it had been placed there before.

As he saw life as a loan, it was also a bridge to an immortal and more magnificent life. Once, his companions went to visit him when he was ill and found him sleeping on a piece of leather. They said to him, "If you wish, you will have better and more comfortable bedding." He replied pointing with his forefinger and looking with his bright eyes at the far distance, "Our home is there. For it, we gather and to it we return. We travel to it and we work for it."

This take on life was not only his point of view, but also his *way* of life. Yazid ibn Muawiyah wanted to marry his daughter, but Abu Ad-Darda refused him and married his daughter to a poor, pious Muslim. People were surprised by this decision, but he explained to them: "What if Ad-Darda (his daughter) had servants and splendours, and she [became] dazzled by the decorations and pleasures of the palace? What then would happen to her religion?"

This was a wise man of upright morals and clear heart. He refused every temptation, and in doing so he did not evade happiness, but escaped to it. As we know, real happiness in his view was to own life, rather than be owned by it. Whenever the needs of people are contained by uprightness, they realise the reality of this life is just a bridge to the eternal abode of moral permanence. Whenever they do so, their share of real happiness is greater. He also said, "It is not better to have much money and many sons, but it is better to have much clemency, much knowledge, and to compete with people in the worship of Allah."

During the caliphate of Uthman (may Allah be pleased with him), Muawiyah was the governor of Syria and Abu Ad-Darda agreed to occupy the position of judge, as per the Caliph's desire. There in Syria, he stood strictly as an example to all those who were tempted by the pleasures of life. He reminded them of the Prophet's asceticism and also that of the early righteous Muslims.

Syria at that time was an urbanised region overflowing with the pleasures and amenities of life. Its inhabitants were annoyed by Abu Ad-Darda's preaching, and felt that he embittered their lives. He gathered once and said to them: "O people of Syria, you are brothers in religion, neighbours at home, and supporters against your enemies. But, why aren't you ashamed? You earn what you don't eat, and build what you don't dwell in, and hope for what you can't achieve. The peoples before you collected cautiously, and hoped confidently, and built firmly, but their gatherings became perdition, their hope became delusion, and their homes became graves. Those were the people of Aad who filled the region from Aden to Oman with wealth and sons." Then, with wide sarcastic smile he would wave his arm to the astonished masses and say sarcastically, "Who will buy the inheritance of

Aad's people from me for two dirhams?"

Abu Ad-Darda's wisdom was faithful, his feelings were pious, and his logic was perfect. In his point of view, worship was neither vanity nor pride, but exposure to the mercy of Allah. Continuous supplication that reminded man of his weakness and the favour of his Lord upon him. He said once of this: "Request the good all your life, and expose yourselves to the mercy of Allah. Allah has fragrance in His mercy which He ushers upon those whom He pleases among His servants. Ask Allah to hide your defects and make your hearts steady and firm in times of trouble."

This wise man was always wary of vanity in worship. Such vanity makes those who have weak faith worship proudly and boast of their worship to others. He once remarked, "An atom's weight of benevolence from a pious man is much better than a mountain's weight of worship from the boaster." He also said, "Don't charge people with unwanted affairs and don't call them to account as if you are their Lord. Guard your own souls. He who follows up the deeds of people will have his grief increased." Abu Ad-Darda did not want the worshipper, whatever his pious rank, to call people to account as if he were the Lord.

His companion Abu Qalabah, also tells us about him: "One day Abu Ad-Darda passed by a man who had committed a sin, and people were insulting him. He stopped them and said, 'If you found him in a ditch, would you not take him out of it?' They said, 'Yes.' He said to them, 'Don't insult him. Praise Allah that He protected you from such an evil.' They said to him, 'Don't you hate him?' He said, 'No, I hate his deed, and if he leaves it, he will be my brother'."

Another key aspect of worship according to Abu Ad-Darda is knowledge and learning. He sanctified knowledge to a great extent and said, "None of you can be pious unless he is knowledgeable, and he cannot enjoy knowledge unless he applies it practically." Knowledge is understanding, behaviour, learning, and life. Because this sanctification is of the wise, we find him claiming that the teacher is like the student in favour, recompense, and position.

He viewed the greatness of life as dependent on goodness before anything else. He said, "Why do I see your scholars going away and your ignorant people learning nothing? The teacher and the student of goodness are equal in recompense and there is goodness in the other people besides the two." He also said, "People are of three types: a scholar, an educated person, and a savage."

As we have seen before, knowledge was intertwined with wisdom for Abu Ad-Darda, and it was key to act on that knowledge. He once said, "The greatest fear of my soul is that it should say to me on the Day of Resurrection, in front of all the creatures, 'O owner, did you know?' And I would reply, 'Yes'. It will say to me, 'What did you do with what you knew?'"

He used to respect scholars and honour them very much. Moreover, he used to pray to Allah saying, "O Lord Almighty, I take refuge in You against the curse of the scholars' hearts." It was said to him, "How could you be cursed by their hearts?" He said, "Their hearts hate me." Do you see, he believed that the scholars' hate is an unbearable curse." Therefore, he implored Allah to grant him refuge.

The wisdom of Abu Ad-Darda (may Allah be pleased with him) recommended fraternity and established human relations on the basis of human nature itself. Thus, he said, "To admonish your brother is better than to lose him. Give your brother advice and be tender with him, but do not agree with his covetousness lest you should be like him. Tomorrow death comes and you will lose him. And how can you weep over him after death when you did not give him his right while he lived?"

The fear of Allah in His servants is the strongest and hardest basis upon which Abu Ad-Darda established the rights of fraternity. He said, "I hate to wrong anyone but I hate more and more to oppress the person who resorts to Allah, the Most High and the Most Great, for help against my injustice."

This was Abu Ad-Darda, the wise man. He was ever the hermit, the worshipper, and constantly seeking Allah. He, who was nurtured by the Prophet ﷺ himself, was a student of the Quran, and the son of early Islam.

(26)

ZAID IBN AL-KHATTAB

The Hawk on The Day of Yamama

One day, the Prophet ﷺ was sat with a group of Muslims, and while they were talking, the Messenger suddenly paused. When he resumed speaking, he said, "Among you there is a man whose molar in Hell is greater than Mount Uhud." Fright and terror appeared upon the faces of all those present; each one of them fearing that he would be the person with this dreadful prophesised end.

Years passed and all those Companions present met their ends as martyrs, except for Abu Hurairah and Ar-Rajjal ibn Unfuwah, who were both still alive. Abu Hurairah was terrified by that prophecy and did not feel comfortable until fate revealed the secret of the unfortunate man: Ar-Rajjal ibn Unfuwah. Ar-Rajjal had in fact left Islam and joined sides with Musailamah the Liar, therefore the prophecy was fulfilled in him.

When Ar-Rajjal was younger, he had visited the Messenger of Allah ﷺ, acknowledged his prophethood and learned the teachings of Islam. Then he went back to his people and did not return to Medina until the death of the Prophet and the appointment of Abu Bakr as Caliph. At that time, Ar-Rajjal told Abu Bakr about the inhabitants of a place called Yamama and their support for Musailamah. He proposed that he be sent to Yamama as an envoy to confirm Islam among them. The Caliph gave him permission.

Ar-Rajjal went to Yamama, but when he saw the enormous support for Musailamah, he became convinced that the people of Yamama would be victorious in battle. And so, his perfidious nature caused him to reserve a place in the prospective state of Musailamah. He immediately apostatised from Islam and joined Musailamah, who promised him a prosperous future.

Ar-Rajjal was more dangerous to Islam than Musailamah himself because he exploited his previous association with the Muslims. He used the time he had spent living with the Messenger in Medina, memorising many verses of the Holy Quran, and his intercession with Abu Bakr all to his advantage. Ar-Rajjal exploited those things, all the while secretly supporting the sovereignty of Musailamah and his false prophethood.

He walked among people saying that he heard the Messenger of Allah say that he had taken Musailamah into partnership, and that when the Messenger ﷺ died, he was worthy of carrying the banner of prophethood and revelation after him. People relied upon Ar-Rajjal's previous relationship the Messenger ﷺ and so the number of Musailamah's supporters increased to a great extent because of his lies. When the news of his betrayal reached Medina, the Muslims were terribly angry, because of the lies he was using to mislead people. The most eager to confront Ar-Rajjal was Zaid ibn Al-Khattab, whose heroism stands out in the books of Islamic history.

Zaid ibn Al-Khattab was the older brother of Umar ibn Al-Khattab (may Allah be pleased with both). He embraced Islam and gained the honour of martyrdom even before Umar. He was the ideal hero, whose motto in life was that actions speak louder than words. His faith in Allah, His Messenger, and His religion was firm. He never stayed away from the Messenger in any setting, and in every battle, he sought martyrdom more than he sought victory.

On the Day of Uhud for instance, at the height of the battle, Zaid was fighting boldly. His brother Umar saw him as his shield fell down within reach of the enemies. Umar cried, "O Zaid, take my shield and fight with it!" Zaid replied, "I want martyrdom as you want it." He continued fighting without his shield with astounding bravery.

As we mentioned before, Zaid (may Allah be pleased with him) was longing to meet Ar-Rajjal, to put an end to his devilish life. In Zaid's opinion, Ar-Rajjal was not only an apostate but also a hypocrite and self-seeker. Zaid was like his brother Umar ibn Al-Khattab in his disdain of hypocrisy and deceit, especially when such lies were aimed at selfish gain and ill purposes. For those ill purposes, Ar-Rajjal committed his atrocious acts. This directly resulted in an increase in the number of Musailamah's supporters and therefore caused a great numbers of deaths in the Apostate Battles. First, he deceived them, and finally he led them to their deaths for the sake of his own vain hopes.

Zaid prepared himself to conclude his faithful life by destroying that impiety, not only in Musailamah's person but also in the more cunning Ar-Rajjal ibn Unfuwah.

The Day of Yamama began gloomy and dim. Khalid ibn Al-Walid gathered the army of Islam. Directed the army into position, he left the leadership of the army to Zaid ibn Al-Khattab. Zaid fought Banu Hanifah (Musailamah's followers), boldly and fiercely. At the beginning, the battle leaned towards the side of the polytheists, and many of the Muslims fell as martyrs. Zaid saw the horror creeping in to the hearts of some Muslims, and so he climbed a hill crying out, "O people! Grit your teeth, fight your enemy and go straight. By Allah, I'll never speak till Allah beats them or I meet Him and then I give my evidence." Then he descended, gritting his teeth in preparation for his foe.

His only hope was to kill Ar-Rajjal, so he began to penetrate the enemy army like an arrow searching for its target, until he saw him. Then he began to attack him from the right and the left. Whenever the deluge of the battle swallowed Ar-Rajjal and hid him, Zaid dived towards him until the waves pushed him to the surface again. Zaid approached him and stretched out his sword towards him, but the furious human waves swallowed Ar-Rajjal again. Then, Zaid dived after him so as not to allow him to escape. At last, Zaid had him by the neck and with his sword, he cut off his head filled with vanity, lies, and villainy. By the death of the great liar, the ranks of its whole army began to fall.

Musailamah and Al-Mahkam ibn At-Tufail were filled with horror. The killing of Ar-Rajjal spread in Musailamah's army like wildfire. Musailamah used to promise them inevitable victory and that he, Ar-Rajjal, and Al-Mahkam ibn Attufail would promulgate their new religion, establishing their state on the day following their victory! Now that Ar-Rajjal was killed, the whole prophecy of Musailamah was seen as a lie, and tomorrow Al-Mahkam and Musailamah would meet the same fate. Thus, the fatal blow of Zaid ibn Al-Khattab caused total destruction to the lines of Musailamah.

No sooner did the Muslims hear the news than they were filled with pride and dignity. The wounded men rose again holding their swords, taking no interest in their wounds. Even for those who were about to die, nothing connected them with life except that very faint light caused by hearing the good news as if in a dream. They wished, if they had any strength to fight with, that they would be able to witness the triumph of the battle in its glorious conclusion. But how could that be? Since the doors of Paradise had opened to welcome them, they were now hearing their names being called to immortality.

Zaid raised his hands towards Heaven, supplicating to Allah and thanking Him for His blessings. Then he returned to his sword and his silence, as he had sworn by Allah not to utter a word until he had completed the victory or gained the honour of martyrdom.

The battle began to lean to the side of the Muslims and their inevitable victory began to approach. At that moment Zaid did not desire a better conclusion to his life than praying to Allah to grant him martyrdom on that Day of Yamama! The wind of Paradise blew to fill his soul with longing, his eyes with tears, and his determination with firmness. He began to fight as if he were searching for his glorious destiny, and the hero fell. So, he died a martyr, magnanimously, gracefully and happily. The Muslim army returned to Medina victorious.

While Umar and the Caliph Abu Bakr were welcoming those who were returning triumphantly, Umar began to search for his homecoming brother with longing eyes. Zaid was so tall that he could be easily recognised. But before Umar had strained his eyes, one of the returning Muslims approached and consoled him. Umar said, "May Allah have mercy upon Zaid, he preceded me in two instances. He embraced Islam before me and gained martyrdom before me, too."

In spite of the victories that Islam won and enjoyed, Umar 'Al-Faruq' (as he was known) never forgot his brother Zaid, and he always said, "Whenever the east wind blows, I smell the scent of Zaid."

The east wind carries the perfume of Zaid (may Allah be pleased with him). But with the later Caliph Umar would give me permission, I would add these words to his great expression: "Since the Day of Yamama, whenever the winds of triumph blow on Islam, Islam finds the scent, the struggles, the heroism, and the greatness of Zaid in those winds!"

Blessings be upon the brothers of Al-Khattab who fought tirelessly under the flag of the Messenger ﷺ. Blessed be the moment that they embraced Islam. Blessed be when they fought and were martyred. And blessings be upon them in the Hereafter.

(27)

TALHA IBN UBAID ALLAH

The Falcon on the Day of Uhud

Of the believers are men who have been true to their pledge to God, from them some have fulfilled their pledges, and some are still in hope of doing so, and they never change at heart. (33:23)

The Prophet ﷺ recited this glorious verse and then turned to his Companions, pointed to Talha and said, "Anyone who wants to please himself by looking at a man walking on the earth who has fulfilled his pledge of martyrdom should look at Talha."

The Companions longed for such announcements from the Prophet ﷺ. Through such words a person could truly feel secure about their destiny and fate. Talha ibn Ubaid Allah was going to live and die as one of those who have been true to their pledge. With such a promise, neither civil strife, nor any kind of lassitude could affect him. The Prophet ﷺ had announced Paradise to him. How then, was the life of such a man who deserved this fine promise?

Talha was trading in the land of Basra, when he met a virtuous monk there. He told him that a Prophet, whose appearance was prophesied by several prophets, was going to appear in the Sacred Land, and his era had already begun. Talha was very much afraid to miss the procession of guidance, mercy, and salvation. And so, when he returned to his homeland, Makkah, after having spent months travelling around, he found a lot of talk taking place. Whenever he met someone or a group of Makkan inhabitants, they would talk to him about Muhammad the Trustworthy. They spoke about the angel sent down to him, and about the mission he was carrying to the people, Arabs in particular.

The first thing he asked about was Abu Bakr. He learned that Abu Bakr had returned with a caravan not long ago, and that he was standing by Muhammad's side, both believing in and defending him. Talha said to himself, "Muhammad and Abu Bakr? By Allah, both of them would never join each other and agree upon falsehood. Muhammad has already reached the age of 40. In all these years we've never heard him speak a single lie. Is it possible that he would now lie about Allah and say, 'He sent me as a prophet and sent an angel to me'? It's something hard to believe."

He quickened his steps in the direction of Abu Bakr's house. They did not talk for long as it was clear to Abu Bakr that Talha longed to meet the Messenger of Allah ﷺ and swear the oath of allegiance to him. So, Abu Bakr accompanied him to the Prophet and he soon embraced Islam, joining the blessed ranks within a heartbeat. That is how Talha became one of the very early converts.

Despite his honourable rank among his clan, his vast wealth, and his successful trade, he had to taste his own portion of the Quraysh's persecution. The task of torturing him and Abu Bakr was given to Nawfal ibn Khuwailid, who was nicknamed 'The Lion of the Quraysh'. However, their persecution did not last long, as the Quraysh soon felt ashamed and began to think about the consequences of their deeds.

Talha emigrated to Medina when the Prophet ﷺ ordered the Muslims to emigrate. After that he experienced all the battles together with the Prophet, except the Battle of Badr, when the Prophet sent him and Sa'id ibn Zaid on an assignment outside Medina. Once they fulfilled their task and were on their way back to Medina, the Prophet ﷺ and his Companions were returning home after the battle.

Talha and his companion felt so sad to have missed the reward of joining the Prophet in his first jihad battle. However, the Prophet ﷺ accorded them peace of mind when he informed them that their reward was exactly like the warrior's reward. Moreover, he gave them a share of the booty equal to the share he gave to each one who had fought in the battle.

Then came the Battle of Uhud, when the Quraysh (with all their might and tyranny) came to take blood revenge for the Day of Badr. They looked to restore their dignity by defeating the Muslims once and for all, a defeat which was thought by the Quraysh to be a simple and predetermined matter. The fierce battle took place, and soon the battlefield was filled with its awful harvest: calamity overtook the polytheists. Then when the Muslims saw them retreating, they laid down their weapons and the archers descended from their posts to collect their share of booty. Immediately and suddenly the Quraysh army turned back to hold the field and tip the balance of the battle in their favour.

The fighting's ferocity and cruelty resumed. The surprise attack had the effect of scattering the Muslim army. Talha saw that the side of the battlefield where the Prophet ﷺ was standing had become the target of the polytheists' concentration. He immediately hurried towards the Prophet. Talha (may Allah be pleased with him) traversed a dangerous path to reach him. He confronted ferocious swords and frantic lances in his struggle to get to the Prophet.

He could see from a distance how the Prophet's ﷺ cheek was bleeding and how he silently suffered. It was then that Talha became enraged. He leapt to the Prophet's defence, as the polytheists drew their swords around them. Talha struck out with his sword to the left and right. He could see the Prophet bleeding and his pains becoming more unbearable. He helped him and carried him away from a hole where his foot had become stuck. He supported the Prophet ﷺ with his left hand and chest, backing up to a safe place, while his right hand fought off the swords of the enemy.

Let Abu Bakr Al-Siddiq describe that scene of the battle for us. Aisha once said: "Whenever Abu Bakr recalled the Day of Uhud he used to say, 'It was Talha's day. I was the first who approached the Prophet ﷺ. He said to me and to Abu Ubaidah ibn Al-Jarrah, 'Watch out, for your brother.' We looked at him, and we could see more than 70 stabs. His finger was cut off. We tried to remedy his condition'."

In all the different events and battles, Talha was always to be found in the forefront fighting in the cause of Allah, redeeming the Prophet's standard.

Talha lived among the Muslim community, worshipping Allah, fighting in His cause, and following Islamic principles, revealed in order to bring people out of darkness into light. After he fulfilled his duties towards Allah, he continued to seek His bounty by expanding his successful business. Talha was in fact one of the wealthiest Muslims. His whole fortune was put in the service of his religion. He spent it without measure, and so Allah increased it for him without measure.

The Prophet ﷺ called him 'Talha the Excellent', 'Talha the Splendid' and 'Talha the Generous' to demonstrate his bountiful generosity. He often gave his whole fortune away; only to find Allah, the Ever-Generous, returning it to him manifold! His wife Suada bint Awf reported: "Once I approached Talha. I saw him worried and asked him, 'What's the matter?' He said, 'The money which I possess is now so abundant that it worries me and makes me feel distressed.' I told him, 'Never mind, I'll distribute it.' He set out to call people and to divide it among them till there wasn't a single dirham left."

On another occasion, he sold his land for a very high price, and when he looked at the pile of money, his tears rolled down and he said, " A man in whose house all that money is to remain for a night and he doesn't know for sure what will happen to him is certainly deceived by Allah." So, he called some of his companions to carry his money with them and they walked through the streets of Medina distributing it until, in the last part of the night, he was without a single dirham of that money. Jabur ibn Abdullah once described his wealth saying, "I never saw anybody giving out so much money without being asked as Talha ibn Ubaid Allah."

He was also one of the kindest toward his kith and kin. He supported them all, though they were great in number. It was once said about him, "He never left an orphan without supporting him and his dependents. He provided for the marriage of the unmarried ones, he provided service for the disabled ones, and paid the debts of the indebted ones." As-Saib ibn Zaid once said, "I accompanied Talha during travels and during times of settlement. I never saw anybody more generous in terms of money, clothes, and food than Talha."

When the infamous civil strife broke out during Uthman's caliphate, Talha actually supported the argument of Uthman's opponents. He stood on their side during most of their quests to achieve change and reformation.

But, did he ever call for Uthman's murder, or even feel pleased by it? Never! If he had known that the civil strife would develop in such a spiteful way, cruelly taking the life of 'The Man of Two Lights', Uthman, he would have resisted it. However, Talha's stance later turned out to be a constant source of conflict in his life after the brutal way in which Uthman was surrounded and killed. Imam Ali had hardly accepted the oath of allegiance from Talha and Az-Zubair at Medina, when they both asked his permission to go to Makkah for Umrah.

From Makkah they both turned to Basra, where a great multitude was gathering to avenge Uthman's death. Finally, things came to a head at the Battle of Jamal, where those calling for revenge met with the party supporting Ali. Whenever Ali thought about this difficult situation facing Islam and the Muslims, he burst into sorrowful tears. He was forced into an unenviable situation.

Being the Caliph of the Muslims, he could not tolerate any revolt against the state or any armed opposition to the established authority. To crush a rebellion of that sort, then, he had to face his brethren, his companions, friends and the followers of his Prophet and his religion. These were people with whom he had so often fought alongside – his brethren in many a battle.

Imam Ali did his utmost to find a way out of the conflict in the hope of saving the blood of the Muslims. Nonetheless, the factors opposing Islam — and they were many — which had met their defeat at the hands of the Muslim state in the days of its great leader Umar, had kindled the civil uprising. These factors continued to stoke the uprising and agitated it, increasing its magnitude.

He wept abundantly when he saw the Mother of the Faithful, Aisha, on her camel at the head of the army which rose to fight him. When he saw Talha and Az-Zubair, the disciples of the Prophet ﷺ, he called to them to come out to meet him, and so they did. They approached him till their horses touched each other. He said to Talha, "O Talha! Did you come with the wife of the Messenger of Allah to use her in your fight while hiding your wife at home?" Then he said to Az-Zubair, "O Zubair! I ask you by Allah. Do you remember the day when the Prophet ﷺ passed you when we were in such- and-such a place, then he said to you, 'O Zubair! Do you love Ali?' You replied, 'Why shouldn't I love my nephew and cousin and the follower of my religion?' He said to you, "O Zubair! By Allah, you will fight him, being unjust to him.'"

Az-Zubair (may Allah be pleased with him) said, "Yes, now I remember, I had forgotten that By Allah, I won't fight you." And so, Az-Zubair and Talha abstained from taking part in this civil war. They abstained as soon as things were made clear. When they saw Ammar ibn Yasir fighting on Ali's side, they remembered the Prophet's prophecy to Ammar: "You will be killed by the unjust party." Talha realised that should Ammar be killed in that war, then he himself would have been part of the unjust party.

Therefore, Talha and Az-Zubair both retreated from the battle, and sadly paid for that retreat with their lives. A man named Amr ibn Jarmuz followed Az-Zubair and killed him while he was praying. As for Talha, he was pierced with a lance by Marwan ibn Al-Hakim, which killed him on the spot. But they both met Allah, pleased and delighted with what they had been endowed by Him: timely insight and guidance.

The murder of Uthman represented in Talha's conscience his "life conflict". Despite the fact that he neither took part in the murder nor agreed to it, he had still supported the opposition against Ali, at a time when it was not obvious that it would intensify into a more serious conflict. When he took his place at the Battle of Jamal amidst the army fighting against Ali, he supplicated, "O my Lord, accept me this day in favour of Uthman until You are pleased."

When they met Ali face to face, both he and Az-Zubair both said they felt illuminated by Ali's words and thereby saw it to be right to leave the battlefield. However, martyrdom had been reserved for them. Did not the Prophet ﷺ once say about him, "He's one of those who passed away. Whoever wants to please himself by seeing a martyr walking on the earth, go let him look at Talha"? So, this was how the martyr met his inevitable fate, and the Battle of Jamal was over. The Mother of the Believers realised that she had made a hasty decision; and so she left Basra for the Sacred House, and then onto Medina, keeping aloof thereafter from the dispute. Imam Ali provided her with all means of comfort and respect.

When Ali inspected all the martyrs of the battle, he set out to pray the funeral prayer upon them, those who fought on his side as well as those who fought against him. When he finished burying Talha and Az-Zubair, he stood saluting them for the last time. He finished his words saying, "I wish to be with Talha and Az-Zubair and Uthman among those whom Allah described thus: *We removed from their hearts any malice therein, as brothers they shall rest upon couches facing each other.*" (15:47)

Then he gazed at their graves with kind and tender eyes saying, "I've heard with my two ears the Prophet ﷺ saying, Talha and Az-Zubair are my neighbours in Paradise'."

(28)

AZ-ZUBAIR IBN AL AWAM

The Prophet's Disciple

Just as it is almost impossible to mention Talha without mentioning Az-Zubair, it is also difficult to mention Az-Zubair without mentioning Talha.

When the Prophet ﷺ was fraternising with his Companions in Makkah before the hijra to Medina, he often sought the company of Talha and Az-Zubair. The Prophet often spoke about them together, for example his famous aforementioned statement: "Talha and Az-Zubair are my neighbours in Paradise."

Both of them were linked to the Prophet ﷺ through lineage. Talha was linked to the Prophet through Murah ibn Kab. And, Zubair was linked to the Prophet through Qusai ibn Kulab. In addition to that, his mother Safia was the Prophet's paternal aunt.

Talha and Az-Zubair resembled each other tremendously in their fates. The similarity between them was also apparent in their upbringing, their wealth, their generosity, their religious solidarity, and their magnificent bravery. Both of them were early converts to Islam. Both of them were among the ten to whom Paradise was promised by the Prophet ﷺ and among the six who Umar entrusted with the duty of choosing the next Caliph after him. Even their destiny was one.

As mentioned, Az-Zubair embraced Islam early on. Indeed, he was one of the first seven who quickened their step towards the faith, and he played his part amongst the blessed early converts at Dar Al-Arqam. At that time, he was just 15 years old, but he was still endowed with guidance, light, and goodness.

He was a horseman and a bold warrior from an early age, to the extent that historians mention that the first sword lifted in Islam was in fact Az-Zubair's sword. In the very early days of Islam, while the Muslims were still few in number and hiding in Dar Al-Arqam, a rumour spread that the Prophet ﷺ had been killed. Young Az-Zubair had hardly heard that rumour when he immediately unsheathed his sword and hurried through the streets of Makkah. First, he went to learn the truth of what had been said, and if it were true, he was intent on attacking the Quraysh until they killed him.

On the high hills of Makkah, the Prophet ﷺ met him and asked, "What's the matter?" A relieved Az-Zubair told him the news. The

Prophet prayed for him there and then, and asked Allah to bestow mercy upon him, and victory upon his sword.

Despite Az-Zubair's nobility among his clan, he still endured the Quraysh's persecution and torment. It was his own uncle who was in charge of his torture. He wrapped him in a mat, set it on fire to let him suffocate, and called to him while he was under the pressure of this severe abuse, "Disbelieve in Muhammad's Lord and I will ward off this torture." Az-Zubair, who was no more than a young man at that time, replied with great defiance, "No! By Allah, I won't return to polytheism ever again."

Thereafter, Az-Zubair emigrated to Abyssinia twice, in both the first and second migrations. Then, he returned to take part in the many battles alongside the Prophet ﷺ. No raid or battle ever missed his presence. The war wounds on his body were plenty, and they were like medals that each spoke of Az-Zubair's heroism.

Let us listen to one of his companions, who once saw and described these medals: "While accompanying Az-Zubair in one of his journeys, I saw his body spotted with sword scars. His chest was like hollow eyes due to the variety of stabs and wounds. I said to him, 'I've seen on your body what I've never seen before.' He replied, 'By Allah, I haven't received one of them except while I was with the Prophet ﷺ and in the cause of Allah'."

During the Battle of Uhud (after the army of the Quraysh had retreated towards Makkah), the Prophet ﷺ assigned him and Abu Bakr to follow the Quraysh's army. They were tasked with chasing them away, so they would realise how strong the Muslim party was and would not think of reattacking Medina. Abu Bakr and Az-Zubair led 70 Muslims in their pursuit. Although they were chasing a victorious army, the military skill used by Al-Siddiq and Az-Zubair, made the Quraysh think that they had overestimated the losses of the Muslim party. They thought that the powerful front row, whose strength Az-Zubair and Al-Siddiq successfully demonstrated, was nothing other than the advance guard of the Prophet's army, which seemed to approach in order to launch a terrible pursuit. The Quraysh hastened away and quickened their pace towards Makkah.

On the Day of Yarmuk, Az-Zubair was an army in himself. When he saw most of the warriors under his command moving backwards as they saw the huge advancing Roman "mountains", he cried, "Allahu akbar! Allah is the greatest!" With his sharp sword, he burst alone into those advancing "mountains", then retreated, and again penetrated the same terrifying rows with his sword in hand, never hesitating.

May Allah be pleased with Az-Zubair, who was so much in love with martyrdom, and ready to die for Allah's cause. He said, "Talha gives his sons names of the prophets and he knows there is no prophet after Muhammad ﷺ. But I give my sons the names of martyrs, and may they die as martyrs!"

In this way he named one son Abdullah as a good omen, after the martyred Companion Abdullah ibn Jahsh; another he named Al-Mundhir after Al-Mundhir ibn Amr; another he named Urwah after Urwah ibn Amr; another he called Hamza after Hamza ibn Abdul Muttalib; another he called Jafar after Jafar ibn Abu Talib; another he called Musab after Musab ibn Umair; and another he called Khalid after Khalid ibn Sa'id. In this way he exclusively chose the names of martyrs for his sons, hoping that they too would die as martyrs, like their namesakes.

It is mentioned in his biography that he never held a governorship, nor an official post, but he would always fight in the cause of Allah. His merit as a warrior can be seen in his total self-reliance and his complete self-confidence. Even if 100,000 warriors were to join him in combat, you would still see him fighting as if standing alone on the battlefield, and as if the responsibility of victory rested on him alone.

He saw his uncle Hamza on the Day of Uhud, when the polytheists had mutilated his corpse dreadfully. He stood in front of him like a high firm rooted mountain, gritting his teeth and gripping his sword tightly. He had nothing in mind except a horrible revenge. Soon, however, a divine revelation prohibited the all the Muslims from such an act.

Az-Zubair would remember his uncle often though, as he did during the siege of Banu Quraidhah. When the siege continued without their surrender, the Prophet ﷺ sent him with Ali ibn Abu Talib to break the stalemate. There in front of the unsurmountable fortress he stood and repeated several times, "By Allah! We will taste what Hamza tasted or we will open their fortress." Then they two alone threw themselves into the fortress. With admirable determination, they were able to terrify the besieged inside into opening the gates. Such was his honour and prestige on the battlefield.

His share of the Prophet's love and appreciation was great. The Prophet ﷺ was so proud of him that he said, "Every prophet has a disciple, and my disciple is Az-Zubair ibn Al-Awam." He was not only his cousin and the husband of Asma bint Abu Bakr, but moreover he was powerful, loyal, brave, and generous. He devoted his life and money to pleasing Allah, Lord of all the worlds.

His characteristics were noble, his good qualities innumerable. He managed a successful trade, and his fortune was enormous; however, he spent all of that in the cause of Islam until he died in debt. His trust in Allah was the reason behind his generosity, bravery, and redemption.

Even when he gave up his soul, he asked his son to pay his debt. "If you're unable to pay it, then seek my Master's help." Abdullah asked him, " Which master do you mean?" He answered, "Allah. He is the best Guardian, the best Helper." Abdullah said afterwards, "By Allah I never fell into trouble because of his debt. I only said, 'O Master of Zubair, pay his debt,' so He did."

At the Battle of Jamal, and in the same way previously mentioned about Talha, Az-Zubair finally met his end. After he saw it right to refrain from fighting, a group of those who had been keen to stoke the flames of civil strife followed him. A treacherous murderer stabbed him while he was praying and standing between the hands of Allah.

The murderer went to Imam Ali, thinking that he would be announcing to him good news when telling him about his attack upon Az-Zubair. The man put a sword into Ali's hands, which he had stolen from Az-Zubair after committing his crime. When Ali knew that Az-Zubair's murderer was standing at his door asking permission to enter, he shouted ordering that he be expelled and said, "Announce Hell to the murderer of Safia's son!" When they showed him Az-Zubair's sword, Imam Ali kissed it and then cried painfully saying, "A sword whose owner had so long wiped the Prophet's grief."

May peace be upon Az-Zubair in death after his life. Peaceful greeting after peaceful greeting upon the Prophet's disciple.

(29)

KHUBAIB IBN ADIY

A HERO ON THE CROSS!

And now, pave the way for this hero. Come close, and be taught an incomparable lesson of sacrifice. Come and see how Allah's religion built such men. Come and see what glory, what strength, what determination, and what loyalty Khubaib ibn Adiy had. Upon hearing his story, you will remember his name well.

Khubaib belonged to the Aws tribe from Medina, and to the Ansar. Since the day of the Prophet's hijra to Medina and since the day of his belief in Allah, he frequently visited Muhammad ﷺ.

His soul, spirit, and conscience were pure, and his belief was firm. He was described by Hassan ibn Thabut, Islam's poet thus: "He looked like a falcon among the Ansar. Allah endowed him with noble character and good morals."

When the standards of the Battle of Badr were raised, he was there, ever the bold warrior. Among the polytheists he killed with his own sword in battle, was Al-Harith ibn Amir ibn Nawfal. After the battle was over and the defeated remnants of the Quraysh had returned to Makkah, the sons of Al-Harith learned that their father had been killed. They learned the name of his killer by heart: Khubaib ibn Adiy. It was a name they would never forget.

The Muslims returned from Badr to Medina and began building their new community. Khubaib was a true worshipper and a pious devotee. He turned to worship with great fervour - praying at night, fasting during the day, and constantly glorifying Allah, Lord of the Worlds.

One day, the Prophet ﷺ decided to ascertain the Quraysh's next plans, so as to be fully prepared for any new battle or targets they had in mind. Therefore, he chose ten of his Companions to act as scouts. Khubaib was among them, and Asim ibn Thabut was chosen as their leader. The expedition set off towards its destination, until they reached a place between Asafan and Makkah. News of their party reached an area of Hudhail called Banu Hayan. A counter group hastened to them with 100 of their most skilful spearmen. They set out to pursue them and to follow their tracks.

The spearmen almost lost them, but then one of them found some discarded date pits in the sand. He picked them up and, with the impressive tracking skill Arabs were famous for, he glanced at them closely. Then he shouted loudly so that the others could hear him, "They are date pits from Yathrib (Medina). Let's follow them and they will surely guide us." They followed the discarded date pits until they could see in the distance what they were searching for.

Asim, the expedition's leader, felt that they were being chased, so he ordered his companions to climb the high peak of a mountain. Just then, the 100 spearmen approached and surrounded the foot of the mountain and besieged them thoroughly. They asked them to surrender themselves after giving them their word not to hurt them. The ten turned to their leader, Asim ibn Thabut Al-Ansari (may Allah be pleased with them all), and waited for his command. He then said, "As for me, by Allah, I will never let myself fall into the protection of a polytheist. May Allah inform our Prophet about us."

The spearmen then began to throw their spears at them. Their leader Asim was wounded and died there as a martyr. In the same way seven others were wounded and died as martyrs. The rest were then called and promised that they would be safe if they came down. The three descended, Khubaib and his two friends. The spearmen approached Khubaib and his companion, Zaid ibn Ad-Dithinnah, and tied them up. Their third one recognised the beginning of their deception, and so he decided he would rather die there beside his companions. He died where he wished, but it was too late for Khubaib and Zaid to resist, they were tied very thoroughly.

The deceitful spearmen took them to Makkah where they sold them to the polytheists. Some people took Khubaib's companion Zaid ibn Ad-Dithinnah and set out to torture him severely. Meanwhile, the name of Khubaib reached everyone's ears. The sons of Al-Harith ibn Amir, who had been killed in Badr, remembered his name very well and were moved only by their hatred to buy him. Most of the inhabitants of Makkah, who had lost their fathers and leaders in the Battle of Badr, also competed in purchasing him in. They encouraged one another to take revenge on Khubaib and began making plans for his fate to satisfy their spite, not just directed at him, but at all the Muslims.

Khubaib submitted his heart, his whole life, and destiny to Allah, Lord of the Worlds. He turned to His worship with a firm soul. Unruffled and fearless, Khubaib had a divine tranquillity about him. Allah was with him, and he was with Allah. Allah's hand was over him, and he could almost feel His fingers within his chest.

One day, one of Al-Harith's daughters entered where he was kept as a captive at Al-Harith's house. She quickly hurried out, calling the people to see an unbelievable thing! "By Allah, I saw him holding a big bunch of grapes, eating from it while being fettered with iron chains - at a time when there isn't a single grape in Makkah. I can't think of it except as being a blessing from Allah!"

Indeed, it was a blessing given by Allah to His virtuous worshipper, as He gave to Maryam (Mary, mother of Jesus) daughter of Imran before: *Whenever Zakariya entered the sanctuary he found her furnished with provision, he said, "O Mary from where did you get this?" She said. "It is from God, surely God provides who He pleases without measure."* (3:37)

The polytheists brought him the news of the death of his companion Zaid ibn Ad-Dithinnah (may Allah be pleased with him). They hoped thereby to break his nerve. However, they did not know that Allah, the Most Merciful, had invited him into His hospitality, blessing him with divine tranquillity and mercy. They set out to bargain with him over his faith, promising to save his life if he disbelieved in Muhammad and his Lord. But they were like children trying to catch the sun by the mere shot of an arrow.

Indeed, Khubaib's faith was like the sun in its strength, light, and far reach. Like the sun, he shed light upon those seeking light, and warmed those seeking warmth; but the one who approached him in challenge was burned and destroyed. When they lost hope of reaching their desire, they took the hero to face his destiny. They took him to a place called At-Tan'im, where he would be killed.

As soon as they reached this place, Khubaib asked them to allow him to pray two rakahs. They allowed him with the hope that he would make up his mind to announce his surrender and disbelief in Allah, His Messenger and His religion.

Solemnly, peacefully and humbly Khubaib prayed his two rakahs.

He felt the sweetness of faith within his soul, and wished that he could keep on praying and praying. However, he turned toward his killers and said to them, "By Allah, were it not for your thinking that I'm afraid of death, I would have continued praying." Then he lifted his hands towards the sky and said, "O Allah! Count them one by one and then perish them all!" Then he scanned their faces intently and set out singing:

When I am being martyred as a Muslim,
I do not care in what way I receive my death
For Allah's sake.
If He wishes,
He will bless the cut limbs.

It was perhaps the first time in Arab history that they crucified a man, then killed him on a cross. They had prepared a huge cross out of palm tree trunks on which they fixed Khubaib, his limbs tied tightly. The polytheists gathered gleefully to watch his suffering while spearmen prepared their lances.

All that cruelty was intentionally performed slowly in front of the crucified hero. He did not close his eyes, and an incredible stillness shone out from his face. Then spears began to skirmish and swords to tear his flesh into pieces. One of the Quraysh leaders approached him saying, "Would you like Muhammad to be in your place and you be healthy and secure among your kin?"

Only then did Khubaib burst like a thunderstorm, shouting to his killers, "By Allah, I would not like to be among my relatives and sons enjoying all the world's health and well-being, while even a tiny thorn hurts the Prophet."

These were in fact the same great words spoken by Zaid ibn Ad-Dithinnah when he was being killed. The same defiant words Zaid had said just one day before. At that, even Abu Sufyan (who had not yet embraced Islam) had to shake his head and say astonished, "By Allah! I've never seen anybody love somebody else the way Muhammad's Companions love Muhammad."

Khubaib's words were so provocative that the spears and swords began to tear the hero's body to pieces, attacking it manically and cruelly. Not far away from this terrible scene, birds and buzzards were circling, waiting for the butchers to end their task. However, soon they called to one another and gathered, their beaks moving as if whispering amongst themselves. Suddenly they flew away. They smelled the scent of a pious, repentant man, and they became ashamed to approach or hurt him further. And so, the flock of birds flew off into the vastness of space.

When the crucifixion was completed, the group of malicious polytheists returned to their dens in Makkah, while the dead body of the martyr stayed there, guarded by a group of Quraysh spearmen.

When they were first lifting Khubaib onto the palm trunk cross and tying him down, Khubaib had turned his face towards the sky asking his Ever Magnificent Lord, "Allah! We fulfilled the mission of Your Messenger. Inform him in the early morning of what is happening to us." Allah had responded to his prayer. While he was in Medina, the Prophet ﷺ was filled with a strong feeling that his Companions were facing a severe trial, and he could almost see the crucified body in his mind's eye. Immediately, the Prophet sent for Al-Miqdad ibn Amr and Az-Zubair ibn Al-Awam. They mounted their horses and set off across the land rapidly. Allah guided them to their desired destination. They lowered Khubaib's body to a pure spot of ground waiting to shelter him under its moist soil.

To this day, no one knows where Khubaib's grave lies. Maybe that is better and more respectable for him, so that he remains in history's memory alone as a hero, a hero who died on the cross.

(30)

UMAIR IBN SAD

The Matchless

Do you remember Sa'id ibn Amir? That steady worshipper who was forced by the Commander of the Faithful Umar to accept the governorship of Syria? We spoke about him in the first part of this book, and we saw the wonders of his asceticism, his renouncement of all worldly pleasure, and his piety. But now we will meet a brother of his, almost his twin in terms of greatness of soul.

That man is Umair ibn Sad. He was nicknamed 'The Matchless' by the Muslims. What kind of man deserves that title? A title agreed on by the Prophet's Companions - with all their merit, enlightenment, and intellect? Let's find out.

Umair's father was Sad, the reciter (may Allah be pleased with him). He witnessed the Battle of Badr with the Messenger of Allah ﷺ and all the events that followed, staying loyal to his oath till he passed away as a martyr in the Battle of Al-Qadisiyah[1].

He brought his son with him to the Prophet ﷺ to swear the oath of allegiance and to embrace Islam. From that day, Umair became a true worshipper. He often dwelled at Allah's mihrab (prayer niche), and preferred to shy away from fame, withdrawing only to the tranquillity and calmness of the shadows.

It was impossible to find him in the front row of life, unless it was the front row of prayer or jihad. In prayer, he stationed himself in front to be granted the reward of the highest in faith; and in jihad he hastened to the front in hope of being one of the martyrs. Other than that, he was dedicated to quietly attaining righteousness, piety, and virtue. He was a devotee to Allah, and hoped only to be accepted as a faithful returner to Him.

Allah blessed him with his companions' love for him. He was the delight of their eyes and the darling of their hearts. That was because of his firm belief, his pure soul, his calm nature, and his beaming appearance. All

[1] In the Sirah of Ibn Hisham, p.519, Vol. 1: The Halaby Second edition, it was mentioned that Umair's father was actually someone else, who died while the Prophet ﷺ was still alive, before the Battle of Tabuk. But Ibn Sad mentioned in At-Tabaqat Al-Kubrah, Vol. 4, p.324: Beirut Edition, that his father was Sad the reciter, and we hold that opinion.

that made him the joy and pleasure of all those who met or saw him.

No person or thing was superior to religion in his eyes. He once heard Julas ibn Suwaid ibn As-Samit, one of his close relatives, saying, "If the man is truthful, then we've more evil than mules!" By "the man", of course, he meant the Prophet ﷺ. Julas was one of those who had initially embraced Islam out of fear.

When Umair heard that statement, his calm, quiet spirit burst into anger and confusion. Anger because someone who called himself Muslim had insulted the Prophet by this wicked language. Confusion because he was concerned about his responsibility towards what he had just heard and denied.

Should he communicate all that he had heard to the Prophet? What of the privacy of meetings and overhearing conversations? Should he keep silent and leave what he had heard within his breast? How? And where was his loyalty to the Prophet ﷺ, who was sent by Allah to guide them after having lived astray; to illuminate them after having lived in darkness?

However, his confusion did not last long. The truthfulness to himself helped him to find a way out. Umair immediately turned to Julas and said, "O Julas, by Allah, you're one of the most beloved to myself and the last one I would like to see afflicted by something he dislikes. You've now said something that if I spread it around, it would harm you; if I keep silent, I would ruin my religion, and the fulfilment of duty towards religion has priority. So, I'm going to inform the Messenger of Allah what you've said!"

Here, Umair pleased his pious conscience completely. First, he fulfilled the duty of preserving the concept of private talks, and elevated his great noble soul away from the role of a slandering listener. Second, he fulfilled his duty towards his religion and shed light on a suspicious hypocrite. Third, he gave Julas a chance to reconsider his fault and to ask Allah for forgiveness. If he had done that immediately, then his conscience would have found peace, and it would not have been necessary to inform the Prophet ﷺ. However, Julas' pride made him hold to his falsehood. His lips did not make any apology. Umair left him saying, "I will inform the Prophet ﷺ before a revelation makes me a partner of your sin."

The Prophet sent for Julas, who denied and moreover swore by Allah that he had not said those words. However, a verse was revealed that demonstrated clearly the true and false parties: *They swear by God that they said nothing, but they indeed uttered the word of unbelief, and disbelieved after they had become Muslims, and they intended a plot but could not accomplish what they intended and they only showed hostility towards Islam after God and His Messenger had enriched them out of His Bounty, so if they repent it will be better for them, so if they turn away, God will chastise them with a painful chastisement in this world and the Hereafter, and on earth there will be none to protect or help them.* (9:74)

Julas found himself forced to confess his fault and to apologise, especially when he heard the holy verse which accused him directly, promising him at the same moment Allah's mercy if he repented and refrained from that: *So if they repent it will be better for them.*

Umair's action was a blessing for Julas. He repented and his Islamic conduct soon became more righteous than before. The Prophet ﷺ gently held Umair's ear and praised him, "O my boy! Your ear was loyal and your Lord believed you."

You will know by now that the Commander of the Faithful, Umar (may Allah be pleased with him) chose his governors very cautiously. He always chose them from among the ascetic, the pious, and the truthful; often those who evaded power and hesitated to accept it unless forced by the Caliph to do so. Despite his unerring insight and his vast experience, he was very scrupulous in making his decision. He famously said: "I need a man who, if among his clan seems like their prince, he isn't so in reality; and who, if among them seems to be ordinary, but he is in fact their prince. I need a governor who won't favour himself above the other people in terms of clothing, food, or dwelling; who will lead them in their prayers, distribute their dues among them fairly, and rule them justly, never shutting his door leaving their needs and wishes unfulfilled."

According to these strict requirements, he chose Umair ibn Sad to be a governor over Homs. Umair tried to free himself of that task, but the Commander of the Faithful obligated him to accept. Umair asked Allah for guidance and went to carry out his duty. A whole year passed in Homs, and no land tax had reached Medina, nor did a single message reach the Commander of the Faithful. So, Umar called for his scribe, to whom he said, "Write to Umair ordering him to come here."

One day, the roads of Medina saw a dusty, unkempt man, covered in the hardship of travel. He could hardly put one foot in front of the other on the hot sandy ground. On his left shoulder there was a sack and a wooden bowl. On his right shoulder there was a small waterskin filled with water. He supported his thin, weak, tired body with a stick. He turned to Umar's assembly with very slow, heavy steps:

"O Commander of the Faithful, peace be upon you."

Deeply afflicted by his weakness and overexertion, Umar asked him, "What's wrong with you, Umair?"

"Can't you see I'm healthy, with a pure conscience and possessing the whole world?" replied Umair.

Umar asked, "What do you have with you?"

Umair replied, "I've a sack in which I carry my food, a bowl in which I eat, my utensils for my ablution and drink, and a stick to lean on and fight an enemy if he crosses my way. By Allah, the whole world is an obedient slave of my belongings."

"Did you come walking on foot?"

"Yes."

"Didn't you find anyone who would give you an animal to ride on?"

"They didn't offer and I didn't ask them."

"What did you do with what we charged you with?"

"I went to the country to which you sent me. There I gathered all its virtuous inhabitants and made them in charge of levying the taxes, so when they did that, I put the money there where it belongs. If anything had remained, I would have sent it to you."

"Didn't you bring us anything?"

"No."

Umar shouted in happy amazement, "Reappoint Umair." But Umair replied with complete composure, "Those were old days. I won't work for you or for anyone else!"

This scene is not a written drama, nor is it an invented conversation. It is a historical event[2] witnessed by glorious city of Medina, the old

[2] Mentioned in Hiliat Al-Awlia Vol. 1, one of our most fundamental sources.

capital of Islam. Such men were unparalleled, the likes of which we have not seen since.

Umar (may Allah be pleased with him) always said, "How much do I wish to have men like Umair to assist me in ruling the Muslims!" That was because Umair, who had been fairly described by his companions as being 'The Matchless', somehow managed to rise above man's natural weakness for material things. When this great man was destined to face the test of power, his piety was still not affected. Rather it elevated him, beaming and bright.

When he was Governor of Homs, he drew a clear picture of the tasks of a Muslim ruler. How often did his words from the pulpit shake the multitude of Muslims: "Islam is a well-fortified wall and a firm gate. As for the wall, that's justice; and the gate is truth. If the wall is torn down and the gate destroyed, then Islam loses its protective strength. Islam remains well-fortified as long as its reign is mighty. The might of its reign cannot be realised by killing with swords or by slashing with whips; rather by the fulfilment of truth and justice!"

It was by these words that he lived and died, may Allah be pleased with him.

generals of Islam. Such men were unparalleled, the likes of which we have not seen since.

Umar (may Allah be pleased with him) always said: "How much do I wish to have men like Umair to assist me in ruling the Muslims." That was because Umair, who had been fairly described by his companions as being "The Matchless", somehow managed to rise above man's natural weakness for material things. When this great man was destined to face the test of power, his piety was still not affected. Rather it elevated him, beaming and bright.

When he was Governor of Hims he drew a clear picture of the ideal Muslim ruler. How often did his words from the pulpit strike the multitude of Muslims: "Islam is a well-fortified wall and a firm gate. As for the wall, that is justice and the gate is truth. If the wall is torn down and the gate destroyed, then Islam loses its protective strength. Islam remains well-fortified as long as its reign is mighty. The might of its reign cannot be realized by killing with swords or by slashing with whips, rather by the fulfilment of truth and justice."

It was by these words that he lived and died, may Allah be pleased with him.

(31)

ZAID IBN THABIT

The Compiler of Quran

When you read the Holy Quran, chapter by chapter and verse by verse, remember a venerated man called Zaid ibn Thabit. For he was foremost among those who were responsible for compiling the copies we read today.

Zaid was from among the Ansar in Medina. When the Prophet ﷺ reached Medina for his hijra, Zaid was just 11 years old. The young boy embraced Islam together with others in his clan and was personally blessed by a prophetic supplication to Allah.

Zaid's father brought him to take part in the Battle of Badr, but the Prophet sent him back because of his tender age. On the day of Uhud, Zaid again went with a group of others to the Prophet ﷺ, humbly begging to be accepted into any of the veteran ranks. The Prophet was ready to reject them all when one of them, Rafi ibn Khudaij, approached holding a lance and moving it skilfully with his right hand. He then said to the Prophet, "I am a spearman. I can throw very well. Please let me!" The Prophet ﷺ greeted the mature and energetic young man with a delightful smile, and allowed him to join. His peers were emboldened. Samurah ibn Jundub approached next, and he began showing the strength of his hands so much so that the Prophet smiled kindly and also allowed him to join the ranks.

Both Samurah and Rafi were already 15 years old, with strong manly builds. Six of the young peers were left, among them Zaid ibn Thabit and Abdullah ibn Umar. They set out to do their best, humbly begging the first time, weeping the second time, and flexing their muscles the third time. However, they were too young and their bodies were not ready for war, so the Prophet ﷺ promised them to take part in the next battle.

Zaid ibn Thabit finally found his place in battle on the Day of Khandaq, in 5 AH. By this time, he was not only proficient as a warrior, but also as an intellectual. He followed up the Quranic revelation by memorising and writing it for the Prophet ﷺ. He proved himself to be exquisite in terms of knowledge and wisdom. When the Prophet began to proclaim his message to the wider world, he sent messages to kings and emperors. Therefore, he ordered Zaid to get acquainted with some of their languages to communicate more clearly to them, which

Zaid did very quickly.

In this way Zaid ibn Thabit's personality thrived and he occupied a high position in the newly formed society. He quickly earned the respect and honour of his fellow Muslims. Ash-Shabi reported: "Zaid ibn Thabit set out to ride, so Ibn Abbas held the bridle. Zaid said to him, 'O cousin of the Prophet ﷺ, let me pass.' Ibn Abbas replied, 'No, it's the way we treat our ulama (scholars)'."

Qabaisah reported: "Zaid was most superior in the field of judgment, jurisprudence, reciting, and the knowledge of obligatory duties." Thabit ibn Ubaid also reported, "I've never seen a more cheerful man at home, and a more respectable one at his assembly, than Zaid." Ibn Abbas said of him, "The tutors of Quranic recitation among the Companions of the Prophet knew that Zaid was one of those deeply rooted in knowledge."

The Prophet's Companions describing Zaid in this way makes us more acquainted with his character. Destiny would endow him with the honour of one of the most noble tasks in Islamic history: the task of compiling the Quran.

Read: In the Name of your Lord Who created - created mankind from something which clings; Read ! And your Lord is the Most Noble; Who taught by the pen, Taught mankind what he did not know. (96:1-5).

From the moment the Quran was sent down, the Prophet ﷺ recited and proclaimed it. While there was a small blessed group moved by its keen interest in the Quran from the very first day, some of them set out to learn what they could by heart. Others, who were talented in writing, set out to preserve the written verses.

During the course of almost 23 years the Quran was sent down verse by verse, not in order and not as a whole. It was sent as a guide for a young nation, therefore it was revealed to them piecemeal - step by step, day after day. In doing so, Allah guided the daily human conduct of that nation. Revelation in this manner allowed for growth and advancement of normative conduct, and responded constantly to ever changing situations and difficulties.

Reciters and scribes would recite or write down the Quran contemporaneously. Leading them were Ali ibn Abu Talib, Ubaiy ibn Kab, Abdullah ibn Masud, Abdullah ibn Abbas, and the honourable Companion we are talking about right now - Zaid ibn Thabit (may Allah be pleased with them all). During the last period of revelation, the Prophet ﷺ recited the Quran to the Muslims with its chapters and verses all put in a particular order.

After the Prophet's death, the Muslims became busy with the apostate battles. During the Battle of Yamama, the number of reciters who died as martyrs was tremendous. The flames of war had hardly died down when Umar hurried to Caliph Abu Bakr Al-Siddiq (may Allah be pleased with him) and insisted that he compile the Quran quickly before the remaining reciters and scribes of the Quran passed away.

The Caliph asked Allah for guidance and consulted his companions, then he sent for Zaid ibn Thabit and told him, "You're a rational youth, in whom we find no faults." Then he ordered him to begin compiling the Quran, assisted by people of experience in that matter. Zaid began his work, with the destiny of Islam's preservation in his hands.

He went about compiling the chapters and verses from reciters' memories and from the written work - comparing, refuting and investigating until he gathered the whole Quran in the order the Prophet had prescribed. His success was attested to by the Companions' consensus (may Allah be pleased with them). The scholars, reciters, and scribes among them in particular had heard the Quran being recited by the Prophet ﷺ during all the different phases of Islam. Their approval was key.

Zaid once described the difficulty that this honourable task represented: "By Allah, if they had asked me to move a whole mountain from its place, it would have been easier than the task of compiling the Quran which they ordered me to fulfil!" Indeed, to move mountains would have been less daunting to Zaid than making the slightest error in moving a verse or completing a chapter. His conscience and religion could withstand any such error, no matter how small or unintentional it may have been. However, Allah's guidance accompanied him as well as His promise: *Indeed! We are the One Who has revealed the Quran, and We will most surely preserve it.* (15:9) And so, Zaid succeeded in accomplishing his work, his duty, and his responsibility.

This was the first phase of the compilation of the Quran. At that time, the Quran had been compiled and written down in more than one book. Although the difference between these books was merely in pronunciation, experience had proven the necessity of uniting them all in to just one version.

During the caliphate of Uthman (may Allah be pleased with him), the Muslims continued their expansions beyond Medina. Islam received groups of new converts each day, one group following the other in swearing the oath of allegiance. It was becoming more and more obvious what a danger the small variation in the Holy Book might present, especially when different people recited the Quran. Even the dialects of the earlier and later Companions differed.

It was then that Hudhaifah ibn Al-Yaman went with his companions to the Caliph, Uthman, explaining the need to unite the Quran into one definitive version. The Caliph asked Allah for His guidance and consulted his companions. Just as Abu Bakr had sought Zaid's aid before, so too did Uthman. So, Zaid brought all his assistants together with all the different versions of the Quran from the house of Hafsa, Umar's daughter, where they were kept safe. Thereupon Zaid and his comrades restarted their great task.

All those who helped Zaid were scribes and reciters of the Quran. Despite that, when they disagreed - which rarely happened - they always considered Zaid's word to be the final decision.

We can only imagine the tremendous difficulties encountered by those destined by Allah to gather and preserve the Quran when we read it so easily or hear it recited. But, in order to spread a virtuous and precious religion throughout the earth, they took this burden on. In doing so, they finally dispelled the darkness with a clear light: the definitive copy of the Quran as we know it today.

(32)

KHALID IBN SAID

A Fighter from the Foremost Muslims

Khalid ibn Sa'id was born into a very wealthy and power-oriented family. His family lived in luxury, and his father was proud of his influential status among the Quraysh. Khalid descended from Ibn Umaiyah, Ibn Abd Shams and Ibn Abd Manaf.

When the first rays of Islam crept in over Makkah to announce in whispers that revelation had descended upon Muhammad the Trustworthy with a message from Allah, Khalid's heart was revived. He opened his ears to the light of those whispers, and he was heedful of them. He was thrilled as if he had been waiting for this news all his life. Whenever he heard his people talking about the new religion, he would join them and listen carefully with repressed delight. Every now and then, he would participate in the conversation with a word or two that gave impetus to the new religion to endorse its effect and improve its publicity.

If you had seen him in those days, you would have the impression that he was a quiet young man who kept to discrete silence. Yet, beyond this calm appearance lurked a man filled with joy and jubilation.

This young man kept his rejoicing to himself and concealed it from all people. He knew that if his father found out that he harboured all this love, enthusiasm, and support for Muhammad's invitation to Allah's way, he would offer him as a sacrifice to the gods of Abd Manaf. But when our inner selves are full with a certain feeling, it is not long before it overflows. One night, Khalid was in a state of half wakefulness when he saw a vision that was very telling.

Khalid ibn Sa'id saw a vision of himself standing on the brink of a great fire. His father stood right behind him. Strangely enough, his father was incessantly pushing him towards the brink. He wanted to throw him into the burning fire. Then, Khalid saw Allah's Prophet rush to him, and pull him with his blessed right hand away from the burning fire.

When Khalid woke up he knew what he had to do. He hastened to Abu Bakr's house and told him about his clear vision. Abu Bakr said, "Allah chose you for His Mercy. This is the Prophet ﷺ. Follow him closely, for Islam will keep you away from Hell." Khalid hurriedly looked for the Prophet until he found him. Then he asked the Prophet about his message. He ﷺ answered him saying, "Worship Allah alone and join none with Him in worship. Believe in Muhammad, His slave and Prophet; and, finally, abandon the worship of idols which do not hear, see, or have power to either harm or benefit you."

The Prophet expressed his heartiest welcome as he shook Khalid's hand. Khalid instantly said, "I bear witness that there is no god but Allah, and I bear witness that Muhammad is His Messenger." All his joy was released, so much so that even his father found out about his Islam.

On the day that Khalid accepted Islam, only four or five others had done so as well. Sa'id thought that his son's early Islam would expose him to the humiliation and ridicule of the Quraysh people. One of Sa'id ibn Al-As' sons had also become Muslim, and this had been enough to throw doubts upon the credibility of that Sa'id's leadership.

So, he summoned Khalid and asked him, "Is it true that you have followed Muhammad, despite his blasphemy against our gods?" Khalid courageously answered, "By Allah, he speaks the truth. I do believe in him and I will follow and obey him." No sooner had he finished these words than his father leaped on him and beat him ruthlessly. Then, he threw him into a pitch black room in the house, where he was imprisoned. He tortured him with thirst, hunger, and exhaustion. Yet Khalid kept on crying out from behind his bars, "By Allah, he speaks the truth and I do believe in him."

Sa'id realised that this torture was not enough; therefore, he dragged his son to the sun-baked ground and dug a ditch for him between its heavy burning rocks, and kept him there for three days without shade or cover. He had absolutely nothing to drink during those three days. His father gave up all hope that his son would turn back from his faith, so he dragged him back home. There, he continued to try luring him to apostatise from the new religion, threatening him all the while.

This cycle of promise and threat went on for some time, but Khalid was resolute. He said to his father, "I will not turn apostate even if you promise me the world. I will live and die as a Muslim, so help me Allah." Sa'id lost his temper and shouted fiercely, "Get out of my sight, you fool! By Al-Lat, I will not sustain you from now on." Khalid answered, "Allah is the best of those who make provision."

Thus, he left the luxurious house that was full of food, clothes, and comfort. He left it to experience need and deprivation. But, why should he worry when he had his faith by his side? Was he not in full control over his conscience and destiny? Then, why should he be bothered by hunger, deprivation, or even torture? If a man found all he was looking for in the great truth that Muhammad ﷺ was inviting people to believe in, there should be nothing in the whole world that could prove to be more important to him than his inner self, which already belonged to Allah.

Thus, Khalid ibn Sa'id subdued torture with sacrifice and overcame deprivation with faith. When the Prophet ﷺ ordered his believing Companions to embark on the second emigration to Abyssinia, Khalid ibn Sa'id was one of the Muhajirun. Khalid settled there for the time destined by Allah. Then, he returned to his house with his brethren in 7 AH. When they arrived, the Muslims had just finished the conquest of Khaibar. Khalid then settled in Medina at the centre of the new Muslim society.

Khalid never missed a battle. He was always the first to go forth during war. Khalid was always conscientious and disciplined, and he was loved and honoured for it. He respected his conviction. Hence, he refused to hide or bargain with it. For instance, before the Prophet ﷺ died, he assigned Khalid to the post of Governor of Yemen. When he heard the news concerning Abu Bakr's nomination as Caliph and the consensus of allegiance given to him, he left his work and set out for Medina.

He knew that Abu Bakr was an unmatched, righteous, and pious believer. However, he thought that the caliphate was Banu Hashim's right. He believed that Al-Abbas or Ali ibn Abu Talib should have been Caliph. He clung to his belief and did not take the oath of allegiance to Abu Bakr. Notwithstanding that, Abu Bakr held no grudge against him. On the contrary, he kept his love and appreciation for him. He did not compel him to give the oath, nor did he begrudge him for refusing. He was hardly mentioned among the Muslims without the great Caliph justly praising him. In time, Khalid ibn Sa'id actually changed his view on the matter. One day, he broke through the lines in the mosque while Abu Bakr was standing at the pulpit and gave the oath of allegiance to him.

Abu Bakr marched with his armies to Syria and assigned the command of a regiment to Khalid ibn Sa'id. Thus, he became one of the commanders of the armies. But before the troops left Medina, Umar objected to Khalid ibn Sa'id's command and prevailed on the Caliph until he changed his previous order. Khalid heard what had happened, yet his only response was, "By Allah, I was not overjoyed with being a commander, nor was I broken-hearted for being dismissed."

Al-Siddiq (may Allah be pleased with him) hastened to Khalid's house to offer him his sincere apology and to explain his new decision. Then, he asked Khalid which of the commanders of the army he would like to accompany to Syria. He asked him if he would like to be in his cousin's ranks, Amr ibn Al-As, or with Shurahbil ibn Hasana. Khalid's answer reveals his inner piety, for he said, "My cousin is closer to me due to the relation of blood, and Shurahbil is closer to me due to his excellent piety." For those reasons, he chose to be a soldier in Shurahbil ibn Hasana's regiment.

Abu Bakr summoned Shurahbil before the outbreak of the war and told him, "Take care of Khalid ibn Sa'id. Treat him as you would like to be treated if you were in his position. You well know his high rank in Islam. You know that when the Prophet died, he was already his governor in Yemen. I myself assigned him as a commander, then I rescinded my decision. I hope that this revoked order will make him even more pious and righteous, for I think that command is a trial. I gave him the chance to choose his commander and he preferred you to his cousin. If you need the opinion of a pious and true adviser, you must resort to Abu Ubaidah ibn Al-Jarrah first; second, Muad ibn Jabal; and third, Khalid ibn Sa'id. You will definitely find good advice with them. I warn you against acting upon your viewpoint alone and without consulting them first."

In the Battle of Marj As-Sufar, where the Muslims and Romans met in terrible and deadly combat, many lives were lost. Amongst them was a pioneer, who from the days of his youth to the moment of his martyrdom, was characterised by true belief and courageous action. When the Muslims were examining their wounded and martyred on the battlefield, Khalid lay there as he always was - a quiet young man with a look of determination on his face. They all cried out, "May Allah be pleased with Khalid ibn Sa'id!"

(33)

ABU AYUB AL-ANSARI

March Forth, Whether You Are Light or Heavy

The Prophet ﷺ entered Medina and finally concluded his successful hijra. Riding on his camel, the Messenger advanced into the massive crowd which overflowed with enthusiasm and love. People crowded around the camel's halter in competition with one another to offer Allah's Messenger their hospitality and accommodation.

As soon as the procession reached the neighbourhood of Banu Salim ibn Awf, the crowd stood in the way of the procession and addressed the Prophet saying, "O Messenger of Allah, please do accept our hospitable accommodation, for we are influential people who are great in number and wealth. We can also guarantee your support and protection." The Prophet ﷺ gently urged them to loosen its halter and get out of its way, for Allah had already ordered that he stop at a certain place.

The procession advanced to the neighbourhoods of Banu Bayada, then Banu Sa'ida, then Banu Al-Harith ibn Al-Khazraj, then to Banu Adiy ibn An-Najar. The people of every tribe tried to stop the camel and pleaded with the Prophet ﷺ to honour them with his approval of their hospitable accommodation. Yet, the Prophet gave them the same answer, smiling thankfully, "Get out of its way, for it has been ordered by Allah to go to a certain place." Thus, the Prophet ﷺ left the choice of his abode to destiny.

Later, this abode would be of critical importance, for on this land the Prophet's mosque would later be built. Next to this mosque, dwellings made of clay and bricks would be built with nothing inside them but the bare essentials for sustenance and living. But the location of these dwellings was key. They would be inhabited by the inspired instructor and Prophet Muhammad ﷺ, who dawned upon this world to revive its waning spirit. He was sent to bestow honour and peace upon all those who proclaim that their Lord is Allah. Therefore, the Prophet was very careful to leave the choice for the place of his abode to Allah's determined decree.

So, he loosened the reins of his camel and did not pull at them. Then, he set his heart to Allah and supplicated, "Allah, pick and choose for me a place for my abode." The camel knelt down in front of the house of Banu Malik ibn An-Najar. Then it got up on its feet, circled around the place, then went back to the same spot again and knelt down, lowered its neck, and was motionless. The Prophet ﷺ was optimistic and glad as he dismounted. One of the Muslims advanced towards the camel, took the saddle bags and carried them into his house. His face shone with joy and satisfaction as the Prophet himself, who was enveloped with good fortune and blessings, followed him right into his house.

Would you like to know who this happy man was? The man in whose house the Prophet was guest, and the man whom all the people of the city envied for his great fortune? He was the Companion Abu Ayub Al-Ansari, also known as Khalid ibn Zaid, the grandson of Malik ibn An-Najar.

It was not the first meeting between the Prophet ﷺ and Abu Ayub Al-Ansari. They had met before when the Medinan delegation journeyed to Makkah to take the oath of allegiance to the Prophet ﷺ in the famous Second Pledge of Aqabah. Abu Ayub Al-Ansari was among the 70 believers who shook hands with the Prophet and gave him his support and loyalty. It seems that Abu Ayub's great fortune was that his house was chosen for the great Muhajir and Prophet to live in when the Messenger of Allah entered Medina, establishing it as the capital of Allah's new religion.

The Prophet ﷺ preferred to live on the first floor. However, no sooner had Abu Ayub Al-Ansari ascended to his room on the upper floor, than he shook with regret for yielding to the Prophet's wish and accepting to live and sleep above the Prophet. Instantly, he pleaded with the Prophet to move to the upper floor. He prevailed upon him, and the Prophet moved to the upper floor. The Prophet ﷺ stayed there until the mosque was built and his dwelling was built next to it.

Ever since the Quraysh began to fight against Islam, to raid Medina, and to instigate tribes against Allah's light, Abu Ayub became professional in warfare and jihad. This hero was there in Badr, Uhud, Khandaq and the remaining battles and wars. He sold himself, his money, and property to Allah, the Lord of All the Worlds.

Even after the Prophet ﷺ died, Abu Ayub never lagged behind or turned his back on a battle, notwithstanding the hardships and the atrocities they brought with them. The slogan that he sang day and night, secretly and openly was Allah's verse: *March forth, whether you are light or heavy.* (9:41)

He never missed an expedition, but once. He refused to fight in an army whose commander was a young Muslim assigned by the Caliph. Abu Ayub was against this choice. This one and only mistake shook his innermost self, and he was always full of regrets as he repeated, "It is none of my concern who was appointed by Ali." Ever since that slip, he never missed a battle, no matter what. It sufficed him to live as a soldier in the Muslim army, fight under its standard, and defend its sanctity.

When conflict erupted between Ali and Muawiyah, he sided with Ali without the slightest hesitation. He believed that Ali was the rightful Imam who had been chosen by the Muslims. When Ali died and Muawiyah took over the caliphate, the ascetic and pious Abu Ayub held himself aloof. He craved nothing of this world but for a place in the battlefield among the Mujahidun who strive in the way of Allah. Therefore, no sooner had he seen the Muslim army march forth towards Constantinople than he mounted his horse, raised his sword, and galloped towards a long-awaited martyrdom.

It was in this battle that he was mortally wounded. The commander of the army paid him a visit to check up on him. He breathed heavily, and impatiently longed to meet Allah even with just a few minutes left of his life. The commander, Yazid ibn Muawiyah, asked him, "What is your last wish, Abu Ayub?"

Astonishingly, he asked Yazid to carry his body to the furthest point inside the enemy lands and bury him there. He then wanted them to break through the enemy line until they reached his grave, so that Abu Ayub might hear the sound of the galloping Muslim horses clattering over him and would recognise their victory. This may sound like poetic verse, but in fact it happened. Yazid carried out Abu Ayub's will to the fullest extent.

The body of this very great man was buried in the heart of Constantinople – modern day Istanbul. Even before Islam enveloped this part of the world with its light, the Romans of Constantinople looked up to Abu Ayub as something of a saint. Strangely enough, historians say that, "The Romans looked after his grave, visited it, and asked God to send down rain for his sake during times of drought."

Abu Ayub's life was full of the regular tempo of battles. He often had no time to sheathe his sword and take a breath; but still his life was as tranquil and pure as the early morning breeze. He once heard the Prophet ﷺ relate a hadith that he always lived by. The Prophet said, "First, if you perform a prayer, perform it neatly as if it was your last prayer. Second, do not utter a word for which you will have to apologise later on. Third, rid yourself of the hope of having whatever is enjoyed by other people."

Thus, Abu Ayub never spread slander or mischief, he never desired anything, and he spent his life absorbed in worship as if death was always near. When it was time for him to die, he desired nothing of this world but for that single heroic wish: "Carry my body far inside the Roman lands, then bury me there." He believed in victory. He had enough insight to foresee that those distant parts of the world would soon be one of the oases of Islam.

Hence, he wanted to be there at the capital of the country where the final decisive battle would take place and where he could, even from his grave, follow the proceedings of war. He longed to hear the sweeping Muslim armies, the fluttering flags, the neighing of the horses, and the clash of swords. Today, he lies there still, and although he cannot hear such sounds any more, the decree of Allah has been fulfilled upon him. Instead, he hears the magnificent sound of the adhan five times a day, emanating from the high minarets across the horizon:

Allahu akbar (Allah is the Greatest).
Allahu akbar (Allah is the Greatest).

His overjoyed spirit in its eternal and glorious home answers: "This is what Allah and His Messenger had promised us and Allah and His Messenger spoke the truth."

(34)

AL-ABBAS IBN ABDUL MUTTALIB

The Provider of Water for the Two Harams

In the Year of Drought, Caliph Umar, along with a great number of Muslims, went out into a vast open area to perform the prayer for rain. Umar (may Allah be pleased with him) held Al-Abbas' right hand in his own and raised it towards the sky as they supplicated, "O Almighty Allah, we used to ask You for rain for the Prophet's sake while he was alive. O Almighty Allah, today, we ask you for rain for the sake of the Prophet's uncle. So please send down rain on us." The Muslim congregation did not leave until rain poured announcing glad tidings, irrigation, and fertility.

The Companions rushed to embrace Al-Abbas and express their affection for his blessed status saying, "Rejoice! You are now the provider of water of the two Harams."

But, what was the man who was called the 'provider of water' for the Haramain really like? Who was this man for whose sake Umar asked Allah to send down rain, notwithstanding Umar's own piety and high station (all of course known to Allah)? He was Al-Abbas, the Prophet's uncle. The Prophet ﷺ held him in great esteem. His reverence and love for him were inseparable. He always praised his good nature saying, "He is the only one left of my family."

Al-Abbas ibn Abdul Muttalib was the most generous man of the Quraysh. Moreover, he was good to his relatives and maintained the bond of kinship. Like the Prophet's other uncle, Hamza, Al-Abbas was nearly the same age as the Prophet ﷺ, being only two or three years older. Thus, Muhammad and his uncle Al-Abbas were of the same generation. Being relatives was not the only bond that made them close friends. They were tied by the bonds of age and a lifetime of friendship.

Al-Abbas' good nature and excellent manners also complemented the Prophet's standards of judgment. Al-Abbas was excessively generous, almost a sponsor of noble deeds for humanity. He treasured kinship bonds, and cherished his family and relatives. He put himself, his influence, and his money at their disposal.

Moreover, he was an extremely intelligent man. His intelligence was tinged with an expert craftiness. This, along with his high status among the Quraysh, enabled him to avert mischief and abuse against the

Prophet ﷺ when he began to invite people openly to embrace Islam.

As we have mentioned before, Hamza countered both the Quraysh's oppression and Abu Jahl's hostility with his sword. As for Al-Abbas, he treated them with a kind of intelligence that benefitted Islam much in the same way that swords defended the faith. A group of historians mentioned Al-Abbas among those who were last in embracing Islam, for his Islam was not announced openly until the year of the Conquest of Makkah. However, others narrated that he was in fact one of the earliest to submit to Islam, but that he hid his faith.

Abu Rafia, the Prophet's ﷺ servant, said, "I was Al-Abbas ibn Abdul Muttalib's slave when Islam dawned on the family of the house. Thus, Al-Abbas, Umm Al-Fadl and I submitted ourselves to Islam, but Al-Abbas hid his Islam." This is Abu Rafia's statement in which he is bearing witness to Al-Abbas' Islam before the Battle of Badr.

So, even though he most likely an early Muslim, Al-Abbas stayed in Makkah even after the Prophet's hijra. This was a premeditated plan though, which later bore fruit. The Quraysh did not hide their suspicions of Al-Abbas' real intentions, but neither could they find a reason to show hostility to him, especially when he showed nothing but adherence to their way of life and religion.

When the Battle of Badr took place, the Quraysh found their golden opportunity to unveil Al-Abbas' real allegiance. Al-Abbas was a shrewd man though, who immediately detected their evil plots. If Al-Abbas was able to inform the Prophet ﷺ in Medina of the Quraysh's plans, they would still succeed in leading him into a battle which he did not believe in. However, it would be a temporary success which would soon become a devastating upheaval.

The two armies met in combat in the Battle of Badr. The Prophet ﷺ called his Companions saying, "There are men of Banu Hashim and of other clans of the tribe who were forced to march forth. They do not really want to fight us. Therefore, if any of you meet one of them during the battle, I order you to spare his life. Do not kill Abu Al-Bakhtari ibn Hisham ibn Al-Harith ibn Assad. Do not kill Al-Abbas ibn Abdul

Muttalib, for he was forced to go forth in this battle."

Now, the Prophet ﷺ was not favouring his uncle Al-Abbas with a privilege, for it was neither the occasion nor the time for privileges. Muhammad would not intercede on his uncle's behalf if he knew that his uncle was one of the disbelievers. Indeed, if the Prophet had been ordered not to even ask for Allah's forgiveness for his uncle Abu Talib, despite his endless support and sacrifice for Islam, then how could he order the Muslims (who were killing their own disbelieving fathers and brothers in the Battle of Badr) to make an exception for his uncle and spare his life? It certainly does not seem feasible. The only logical explanation is that the Prophet knew his uncle's secret and hidden allegiance and his secret services for Islam. He also knew that he was forced to go forth to the battle. Therefore, it was his duty to save him as far as he was able to.

Although Abu Al-Bakhtari ibn Al-Harith was not Muslim, he won the Prophet's intercession because he refused to take part in the Quraysh's abuse and oppression against the Muslims. Second, he went forth to battle out of embarrassment and compulsion. Was not a Muslim who hid his Islam and supported it openly and secretly in many notable situations more worthy of this intercession? Indeed, Al-Abbas was that Muslim and that helper. Let us go back in time to prove this statement.

In the Second Pledge of Al-Aqabah, 70 men and two women from a delegation of the Ansar came to Makkah during the Hajj season to take the oath of allegiance to the Prophet. They also came to make preparations with the Prophet ﷺ for the imminent emigration of the Muslims to Medina. At that time, the Prophet was keeping his uncle Al-Abbas well-informed about the delegation and the pledge, for he trusted him and treasured his opinion.

When it was time for the secret meeting, the Prophet ﷺ and his uncle Al-Abbas went to where the Ansar were waiting for them. Al-Abbas wanted to test their loyalty and ability to protect the Prophet.

Now, let us hear one of the delegation, Kab ibn Malik, narrate the proceedings of this meeting: "We sat in the ravine waiting for the Prophet ﷺ until he arrived accompanied by his uncle. Al-Abbas ibn Abdul Muttalib said, 'O people of Khazraj, you are well aware of Muhammad's lineage. We have prevented our people from abusing him. He lives here protected and supported by his people and in his own country, yet he prefers to accompany you and emigrate to Medina. So, on the one hand, if you are certain that you will be capable of giving him sufficient help, protection, and safety, then fulfil your pledge to the fullest. On the other hand, if you intend to forsake and thwart him after he has emigrated to you, then you had better show him your true colours now before it is too late'."

As Al-Abbas uttered these decisive words, his eyes were surveying the Ansar's faces in order to trace and observe their reflexes and reaction to his words. The inquisitive Al-Abbas was not satisfied with what he saw. So, he posed an intelligent question: "Describe to me your combat readiness and war strategy." Al-Abbas was astute enough and experienced with the nature and disposition of the Quraysh to realise that war between Islam and disbelief was inevitable, for on the one hand there was no way that the Quraysh would accept to forsake their religion and arrogance. On the other hand, Islam would not yield its legitimate rights to the power of falsehood. The question was, would the people of Medina stand firmly behind the Prophet ﷺ at the outbreak of war? Were they, technically speaking, on the same level of expertise in the tactics of war, attack, and retreat as the Quraysh were? That was what Abbas had in mind when he asked them to describe their combat readiness and war strategy.

The Ansar were as firm as a mountain whilst they listened to Al-Abbas. No sooner had he finished asking this provocative question than the Ansar spoke: "By Allah, we are given to warfare. We are men of soldierly bearing. We were raised on the tactics of war and trained to fight. We inherited excellent warfare expertise from our fathers and grandfathers. We have learned to keep on shooting arrows until the last one. We have learned to stab with our spears until they break. We have learned to carry our swords and strike hard until either we or our enemy is vanquished." Al-Abbas was pleased with their answer, and he replied, "I can tell from what I have just heard that you are masters of warfare, but do you have armour?" They answered, "Of course, we have armour, shields, and helmets."

This was Al-Abbas' part in the Second Pledge of Al-Aqabah. Whether he had already embraced Islam or not yet does not change the fact that his attitude determined his later role in supporting the dawn of Islam. Moreover, it sheds light on his outstanding stout-heartedness. Finally, when the Battle of Hunain took place, Al-Abbas' allegiance was clear. This quiet and compassionate man's heroism projected on to the battlefield and made his Islam apparent in a moment of necessity.

Soon after, the Conquest of Makkah took place in 8 AH. Some of the influential Arab tribes were enraged by the swift victory that Islam had achieved in such a short time. Therefore, the Hawazan, Thaqif, Nasr, Jusham, and other tribes held a meeting to discuss options. They agreed to wage a decisive war against the Prophet ﷺ and the Muslims.

Now, we should not let the word 'tribes' mislead us into underestimating the gravity of the wars that the Prophet ﷺ fought throughout his life. We must not think that they were small-scale skirmishes. On the contrary, these tribal wars, fought at the tribes' strongholds, were far more difficult than ordinary wars. If we bear this fact in mind, we have a more accurate picture of the incredible effort exerted by the Prophet ﷺ and his Companions. It also recognises the value of the victory Islam achieved.

The tribes gathered in endless waves of fierce warriors. There were 12,000 soldiers in the Muslim army alone. But, their unprecedented victory in Makkah had caused pride to creep into the Muslim conscience. Consequently, they said, "We shall not be overcome by a small group."

They depended solely on military power, and pride in their military conquest. These vain sentiments had a shock awaiting them. This shock was a sudden, large-scale defeat shortly after the two armies met in fierce combat. The Muslims at once supplicated to Allah in humiliation and submission. They finally perceived that there was no fleeing from Allah, no refuge but with Him, and no power but His. These supplications flowed throughout the battlefield, tangibly turning defeat into victory.

The glorious Quran descended addressing the Muslims: *...on the Day of Hunain when you rejoiced at your great number but it availed you naught and the earth, vast as it is, was straitened for you, then you turned back in flight. Then Allah did send down His tranquility upon the Messenger and on the believers, and sent down forces which you saw not, and* *punished the disbelievers. Such is the recompense of disbelievers.* (9:25-26).

While the Muslims joined forces in one of the valleys waiting for the arrival of their enemies, the polytheists were already hidden throughout the ravines with unsheathed swords. They wanted to take the initiative. Suddenly, they flung themselves into the battlefield and attacked the Muslims ruthlessly. This blitzkrieg shook the Muslims and made them turn their backs to the battle and run away without even casting a glance at one another. When the Prophet ﷺ saw the chaos that this sudden attack brought to the Muslim lines, he at once mounted his white mule and cried out at the top of his voice, "Where are my people? Come back and fight! I am truly the Prophet! I am the son of Abdul Muttalib!"

At that moment, the Prophet ﷺ stood there surrounded by Abu Bakr, Umar, Ali ibn Abu Talib, Al-Abbas ibn Abdul Muttalib, his son Al-Fadl ibn Al-Abbas, Jafar ibn Al-Harith, Rabuiah ibn Al-Harith, Usama ibn Zaid, Ayman ibn Ubaid and a few other Companions.

There was also a woman who was raised to a high station among those men and heroes, the pregnant Umm Sulim bint Milhan. When she saw the chaos and confusion that the Muslims had fallen into, she mounted her husband Abu Talha's camel (may Allah be pleased with them both) and hastened towards the Prophet ﷺ. When her baby moved in her womb, she took off her outer garment and pulled it tight around her belly. As soon as she reached the Prophet ﷺ, she gave him her dagger. The Prophet smiled and asked, "Why do you give the dagger to me, Umm Sulim?" She answered, "You are dearer to me than my own father and mother. Kill those who turned their backs on you as you do your enemies, for they deserve the same punishment." The Prophet's face was calm, for he had strong faith in Allah's promise, and he said, "Allah sufficed us against them and has been good to us."

In those difficult moments, Al-Abbas was next to the Prophet ﷺ. In fact, he followed him like his shadow, holding the halter tightly and defying death. The Prophet ordered him to cry out at the top of his voice, for he was a stout and loud-voiced man, saying, "Come back and fight, O Ansar people! Come back, for you took the oath of allegiance to

Allah and His Prophet." His voice sounded throughout the battlefield as if it was both the caller and warner of destiny.

As soon as those terrified and dispersed Muslims heard his voice, they answered in one breath, "Here I am at your service. Here I am at your service." They flung themselves back into the battlefield. Dismounting their frightened horses and camels, they ran with their shields, swords, and bows as if drawn by Al-Abbas' voice. Once again, the two armies met in fierce combat. The Prophet ﷺ cried out, "Now it is time for fierce fighting." It truly was a ferocious fight. The bodies of Hawazan and Thaqif rolled down the battlefield. Allah's warriors finally defeated the warriors of the idol, Al-Lat. Allah soon sent down His tranquillity on the Prophet and the believers in the aftermath of the battle.

The Prophet ﷺ loved his uncle Al-Abbas dearly, to the extent that he could not sleep when the Battle of Badr first lay down its burden and his uncle was captured by the Muslims. Although this was well before his public acceptance of Islam, the Prophet ﷺ did not try to hide his feelings. When he was asked about the reason for his sleeplessness, despite his sweeping victory, he said, "I heard Al-Abbas moan in his fetters." As soon as a group of Muslims heard the Prophet's words, they rushed to where the captives were, untied Al-Abbas, and returned to the Prophet saying, "O Prophet, we loosened Al-Abbas's fetters a little." But why should Al-Abbas alone enjoy this privilege? Consequently, the Prophet ordered them, "Go and do that to all the prisoners."

Indeed, the Prophet's love for Al-Abbas did not mean that he should receive special treatment that distinguished him from other captives. When it was decided that a ransom would be taken in exchange for the captives' freedom, the Prophet ﷺ asked his uncle, "O Abbas, pay the ransom for yourself and your nephew Aqil ibn Abu Talib, Nawfal ibn Al-Harith and your ally, Utbah ibn Amr and the brothers of Banu Al-Harith ibn Fahr, for you can afford it."

Al-Abbas wanted to be set free without paying a ransom, saying, "O Messenger of Allah, I was a Muslim but my people forced me to go forth in this battle." But the Prophet ﷺ insisted on it. The glorious Quran descended to comment on this incident saying, *O Prophet! Say to the captives that are in your hands: If Allah knows any good in your hearts,*

He will give something better than what has been taken from you, and He will forgive you, and Allah is Oft-Forgiving, Most Merciful. (8:70).

Hence, Al-Abbas paid the ransom for himself and his friends to return to Makkah. From that point onwards the Quraysh lost their influence over him and their benefit from his insight and guidance. Therefore, Al-Abbas took his money and luggage and joined the Prophet in Khaibar, so as to have a place in the ranks of Islam and the believers. The Muslims loved and honoured him, especially when they realised how much the Prophet ﷺ loved and honoured him. Muhammad ﷺ once said, "Al-Abbas was like a twin brother to my father. Consequently, if anyone annoyed Al-Abbas, it would be as though he personally annoyed me."

On Friday, the 14th of Rajab, 32 AH, the people of Al-Awali in Medina heard a crier calling out, "May Allah have mercy on whoever saw Al-Abbas ibn Abdul Muttalib." They realised at once that Al-Abbas had died. An unprecedented congregation of people, the likes of which Medina had not experienced before, accompanied the funeral procession to the graveyard. The Commander of the Faithful, Uthman (may Allah be pleased with him) performed the funeral prayer. The body of Al-Abbas was laid to rest in Baqi cemetery. He sleeps comforted to this day among the faithful who have been true to their covenant with Allah.

(35)

ABU HURAIRAH

The Memory in the Era of Revelation

A person's intelligence can often reckon against them, and those who possess extraordinary gifts often pay a price in place of thanks or reward. The noble Companion Abu Hurairah was one of those people, and his unusual gift was his strong memory.

He (may Allah be pleased with him) was skilled in the art of listening and preserving what he heard. He would listen, understand, and memorise. He would hardly forget one word for the rest of his life. That is why he was able to memorise and narrate more Prophetic traditions (hadiths) than any of the other Companions of the Messenger ﷺ.

During the period of Al-Wadin, the writers who specialised in telling lies about the Messenger of Allah ﷺ misused Abu Hurairah's wide reputation for narrating about the Prophet. Whenever they fabricated a hadith they used to say, "Abu Hurairah said...". In doing so, they tried to call Abu Hurairah's reputation as a narrator into question. However, because of the extraordinary efforts of people who devoted their lives to preserving the Prophetic Hadith, Abu Hurairah was saved from the evil intent of these lies, and their falsehood was rejected.

We so often hear a preacher, lecturer or Friday sermon using the common expression, "Narrated by Abu Hurairah (may Allah be pleased with him): The Messenger of Allah ﷺ said...". When we hear his name in that form, or read it repeatedly in books, it is important to know that you are mentioning a Companion with one of the most interesting characters. His ability to listen was beyond compare. He memorised countless traditions and wise instructions from the Prophet ﷺ, thanks to his great fortune and incomparable gift.

He was also a Companion who embodied the Islamic revolution and all the tremendous change that it brought about. He changed from a workman to a master, from a lost man in the crowd to a stand-out imam, from a worshipper of stones to a believer in Allah. He said of himself: "I was brought up as an orphan, and I emigrated as a poor man. I worked for Busrah bint Ghazwan for my daily food. I used to serve them when they dismounted, and walked near them when they rode. And now Allah has married her to me. All praise to Allah Who made the religion our support and made Abu Hurairah an imam."

It was 7 AH when he went to the Prophet ﷺ in Khaibar, and embraced Islam there. From the time he pledged his allegiance to the Prophet, he did not part from him except to sleep. Thus, he spent four years living alongside the Messenger of Allah ﷺ, from the time he embraced Islam till the time the Prophet died. Those four years were filled with virtuous words, deeds, and much attentive listening.

By virtue of his good nature, Abu Hurairah was able to play a prominent role in serving the religion of Allah. There were many war heroes among the Companions. There were many jurisprudents, propagators of the faith, and teachers, but the milieu lacked scribes. In that time, most societies - not only the Arabs – were not very concerned with writing things down. Keeping records was not yet a sign of a developed society. It was the same even in Europe not so long ago. Most of its kings, with Charlemagne at the top of the list, could not read or write, although they were intelligent and capable regardless.

Let us go back to our study of Abu Hurairah. He realised that the new society that Islam was building would need to preserve its legacy and teachings. There were scribes among the Companions who used to write, but they were few. Besides, some of them had no free time to be able to write every hadith that the Messenger uttered.

Abu Hurairah was not a scribe, but he learned things by heart. He had the necessary free time to invest in such a project, for he had no land to tend and no commerce to look after. Believing that he had embraced Islam quite late, he intended to make up for lost time by being by the Messenger's side as much as possible. Besides, he himself knew the gift Allah had bestowed on him - his broad, retentive memory, which only became stronger after the Messenger himself invoked Allah to bless it for him.

Thus, he devoted himself and his precise memory to memorising the hadiths and instructions of the Messenger of Allah ﷺ. When the Prophet died, Abu Hurairah kept narrating his traditions, which made some Companions wonder how he could know all those hadiths? When did he hear them? Abu Hurairah (may Allah be pleased with him) shed light on this phenomenon, as if defending himself against the doubts of some of the Companions.

He said: "You say that Abu Hurairah narrates much about the Prophet ﷺ and that the Muhajirun who preceded him to Islam do not narrate those traditions. But my friends among the Muhajirun were busy with their contracts in the market, and my friends among the Ansar were busy with their lands. I was a poor man, always sitting with the Messenger of Allah, so I was present when they were absent, and I memorised if they forgot. Besides, one day the Prophet ﷺ said, 'Whoever spreads his garment till I finish my speech, then collects it to his chest, will never forget whatever I've said!' Therefore, I spread my clothes and he directed his speech to me, then I collected it. By Allah, I did not forget what he said to me later on. By Allah, I would have narrated nothing at all, but for a verse of Allah's Book: *Surely those who conceal the manifest Revelations and the guidance which We have revealed, after We have made it clear for the people in the Book, those it is who shall be cursed by God and by those who curse.*" (2:159)

This was how Abu Hurairah explained his unique ability to narrate so many hadiths. Firstly, he had the time to accompany the Prophet more than anyone else. Secondly, he had a strong memory blessed by the Messenger so it became stronger. Thirdly, he did not narrate because he was fond of narrating, but because spreading those traditions was his responsibility. He did not want to be a concealer of good, nor would he be negligent of his duties.

For these reasons he kept narrating, and nothing could stop or hinder him, even when Umar told him, "Stop narrating about the Messenger of Allah, or I'll send you to the land of the Daws" (the land of his people). The Commander of the Faithful was not accusing Abu Hurairah, but merely trying to promote his campaign at the time (to encourage Muslims to read and memorise nothing but the Quran, so that it would settle in their hearts and minds). The Quran is Islam's guidebook and constitution. Narrating about the Messenger of Allah ﷺ abundantly, especially in the years that followed his death when the Quran was being compiled, caused unnecessary confusion. That is why Umar used to say, "Get busy with the Quran; it is Allah's words". He also used to say, "Narrate a little about the Messenger of Allah but for what can be followed."

When he sent Abu Musa Al-Ashari to Iraq, he said to him, "You are going to people where you can hear the sound of the Quran in their mosques as if it were a drone of bees. Let them do what they are doing and don't occupy them with traditions. I'm your partner in this." The Quran had been compiled in a warranted way, so that nothing had crept into it. But Umar could not guarantee that some traditions were not forged to tell lies about the Messenger of Allah ﷺ, and thus harm Islam. Hence, his caution.

Abu Hurairah appreciated Umar's point of view, but he was also sure of himself and his honesty. He did not want to conceal anything of the traditions or knowledge that he thought would be a sin to conceal. Hence, whenever he found a chance to unload the traditions he had heard or understood from his breast, he did so.

Once, Marwan ibn Al-Hakam wanted to examine Abu Hurairah's memorising ability. Marwan invited him to sit with him and asked Abu Hurairah to narrate about the Messenger of Allah ﷺ while a scribe sat behind a screen and was told to write whatever Abu Hurairah said. After a year, Marwan invited him once again and asked him to narrate the same traditions the scribe had recorded. Abu Hurairah had not forgotten a single word!

He used to say about himself, "No one among the Companions of the Messenger of Allah ﷺ narrates about him more than I do, except Abdullah ibn Amr ibn Al-As. He used to write, but I didn't."

Imam Ash-Shafi (may Allah be pleased with him) said about him, "No one in his period was more capable of narrating traditions with such a memory than Abu Hurairah." Al Bukhari (may Allah be pleased with him) said, "Almost 800 or more Companions, followers (the generation after the Companions) and people of knowledge narrated through Abu Hurairah." It was as if Abu Hurairah was a school in himself.

Abu Hurairah was a diligent worshipper who would take turns with his wife and daughter to pray throughout the night. He prayed one third of the night, his wife another third, and his daughter the other third. Thus, not one hour of the night passed in Abu Hurairah's house without prayers.

In order to be free to accompany the Messenger of Allah ﷺ, he endured the cruelty of hunger like no other. He used to talk about the times when hunger was so intense that he would tie a stone on his stomach, and lay on his (liver's) side to stave off hunger. He did so once in the mosque while twisting in so much pain that some of his friends thought that he might be epileptic (although he was not).

When he embraced Islam, he had only one persistent problem that would not let him sleep. That problem was his mother, for she refused to embrace Islam. Not only that, but she also used to hurt her son by speaking ill of the Messenger of Allah ﷺ. One day she spoke to Abu Hurairah about the Prophet in a way that he hated. So, he left her in tears, and went to the Messenger's mosque.

Let us listen to him narrate the rest of the story: "I went to the Messenger of Allah crying and said, 'O Messenger of Allah, I used to call Umm Hurairah to Islam, and she used to refuse. Today, I called her, but she spoke to me about you in a way that I hated. Invoke Allah to guide Umm Hurairah to Islam.' So the Messenger of Allah ﷺ said, 'O Allah, guide Umm Hurairah.' Then I ran out to give her the good news about the Messenger of Allah's invocation to Allah. When I arrived at the door, I found it closed, and I heard the sound of water. She called, 'Stay where you are, Abu Hurairah.' Then she put on her shift and veil and she came out saying, 'I bear witness that there is no god but Allah and that Muhammad is His slave and Messenger.' So, I hurried to the Messenger of Allah ﷺ crying out for joy as I had cried for sadness and I said, 'Here is good news, O Messenger of Allah. Allah has answered your invocation. Allah has guided Umm Hurairah to Islam.' I added, 'O Messenger of Allah, invoke Allah to make all the believers love me and my mother.' He said, 'O Allah, make every believer love this slave of Yours and his mother'."

Abu Hurairah led the life of a worshipper and fighter. He did not miss a battle or a pious deed. During the caliphate of Umar ibn Al-Khattab (may Allah be pleased with him), he made him governor of Bahrain. Umar, as we know, used to call his rulers sternly to account. If he made one of them governor when he had two garments, on the day he ceased to govern, he should still own no more than those two garments, and it would be better to leave office with only one! But if he left office with any display of wealth, he would not escape Umar's reckoning, even if the source of his fortune was halal.

When Abu Hurairah was made governor of Bahrain, he saved some money from halal sources. However, Umar knew of it and invited him to Medina. Let Abu Hurairah narrate the quick conversation that took place between them: "Umar said to me, 'O the enemy of Allah and His Book, did you steal the money of Allah?' I said, 'I am not the enemy of Allah or His Book. I am the enemy of their enemy. Besides, I am not the one who steals the money of Allah!' He said, 'Then how did you gather 10,000?' I said, 'I had a horse that had foaled repeatedly.' Umar said, 'Put [the money] in the Bait Al-Mal (the treasury)'."

Abu Hurairah gave the money to Umar and raised his hands towards the sky saying, "O Allah, forgive the Commander of the Faithful." After a while Umar called Abu Hurairah and offered him the governorship again. However, he refused and apologised. Umar asked why. Abu Hurairah said, "So that my honour would not be at stake, my money would not be taken, and my back would not be beaten." He added, "I'm afraid I would judge without knowledge or speak without patience."

One day, his yearning to meet Allah intensified. While his visitors were invoking Allah to cure him of his disease, he was imploring Allah saying, "O Allah, I love to meet You, so love to meet me." So it was, in 59 AH, that Abu Hurairah died at the age of 78. His tranquil body was buried in a blessed place among the revered inhabitants of Al-Baqi cemetery.

Returning from his funeral, the people kept reciting many of the traditions that he had taught them about the noble Messenger. One of the recent Muslims asked his friends, "Why was our deceased sheikh called Abu Hurairah?" His knowing friend answered, "In the pre-Islamic time his name was Abd Shams. When he embraced Islam, the Messenger called him Abdur Rahman. He used to be sympathetic towards animals. He had a cat that he used to feed, carry, clean, and shelter, and it used to accompany him as if it were his shadow. That is why he was called Abu Hurairah, which means father of the small cat. May Allah be pleased with him."

(36)

AL-BARA IBN MALIK

Allah and Paradise

Al-Bara was one of two brothers who lived for the cause of Allah and who both pledged and fulfilled their allegiance to the Messenger of Allah ﷺ.

The first brother was Anas ibn Malik, the servant of the Messenger of Allah ﷺ. His mother, Umm Sulaim, took him to the Messenger at the age of ten and said, "O Messenger of Allah, this is Anas, your lad. He will serve you; invoke Allah for him." The Messenger kissed him between his eyes and invoked a blessing upon him that led his long life towards good and blessing. He said, "O Allah, let him have plenty of money and sons. Bless him and let him enter Paradise." So, he lived for 99 years, during which Allah bestowed upon him plenty of sons and grandsons, and provided him with a spacious garden that gave fruits twice a year!

The second of these brothers was Al-Bara ibn Malik, who led a brave life. His motto was "Allah and Paradise!" Whoever would see him fighting in the cause of Allah would be in awe, for when Al-Bara fought he was not seeking victory, but martyrdom. For this reason, he missed neither a battle nor an expedition.

One day his brothers went to visit him whilst ill. He read their faces and reassured them, "I guess you're afraid I will die in bed. No, by Allah, He will not deprive me of martyrdom." Allah realised his hopes, as Al-Bara did not die in bed, but was martyred in one of the most glorious battles of Islam.

Al-Bara's bravery on the Day of Yamama revealed his true self. This was a hero whom Umar ibn Al-Khattab forbade to be a leader, because his boldness and quest for martyrdom made it too risky for him to lead others.

On the Day of Yamama, the Muslim armies were preparing to fight under the leadership of Khalid. Al-Bara eagerly awaited his leader's order to advance. His sharp eyes scanned the battlefield as if searching for the his final resting place. Nothing preoccupied him more in the world than this aim. With the edge of his sword, a harvest of the polytheists were cut down. It was at the end of this battle though that he too was struck down.

When Khalid shouted, "Allahu Akbar," the ranks burst forth to their fate, along with Al-Bara ibn Malik. He began tackling Musailamah's followers, and they fell like autumn leaves under his sword. Musailamah's army was neither weak nor small, but was in fact the most dangerous army of the apostasy. With its numbers, equipment, and the defiance of its fighters, the army posed an extremely serious challenge. They answered the Muslims' attack with such an aggressive defence that they were poised to gain the upper hand.

Just then, some sort of anxiety took hold in the Muslim ranks. Their leaders started giving words of encouragement from their horses, and they were reminded of Allah's promise. Al-Bara had a loud and clear voice. His leader Khalid called him saying, "Speak, Bara!" So, Al-Bara shouted, "O people of Medina! Today you have no Medina, but it's Allah and Paradise!" These words demonstrated the spirit of their speaker and revealed his true character. They were reminded to not even think of Medina, where they had left their houses, women, and children behind. This was because, if they were defeated on that day, there would not be any Medina to return to.

Al-Bara's inspired words spread with instant effect. It was not long before the battle returned to its former advantage. As the Muslims headed towards certain victory, Al-Bara was walking with his brothers whilst carrying the standard of Muhammad ﷺ. The polytheists withdrew and fled, seeking refuge within a big garden which they entered. The Muslims' enthusiasm abated; it seemed that it was now possible to change the battle's outcome by this trick that Musailamah's followers and army had resorted to. Just then Al-Bara ascended a high hill and cried, "O Muslims, carry me and throw me over to them in the garden."

As we have said, he was not looking for victory but martyrdom. This plan, he thought, would be the best way to die. If he was thrown into the garden, he would open its gate from the inside for the Muslims, and at the same time his body would be torn into pieces by the polytheists' swords. Also at the same time, also, the doors of Paradise would be opening to him.

However, Al-Bara did not wait for his people to carry and throw him. He climbed the wall by himself, threw himself inside the garden, opened the gate, and the armies of Islam rushed in. But Al-Bara's dream did not come true: neither did the polytheists swords kill him, nor did he die as he wished.

Abu Bakr (may Allah be pleased with him) spoke the truth when he said, "Strive for death and you will live!" On that day the hero received from the polytheists' swords over 80 strikes, over 80 wounds that caused Khalid ibn Al-Walid to continue supervising his nursing and care for an entire month.

All of this was not what he wished. But it did not make Al-Bara hopeless. He waited for another battle. The Messenger of Allah ﷺ had prophesied that his supplication to Allah would be answered. He only had to keep invoking Allah to grant him martyrdom, and he did not have to be in a hurry, for every matter there is a decree.

After Al-Bara's wounds from Yamama had healed, he rushed to his next expedition with the Muslim armies. Two empires continued to persecute their Muslim subjects - the Romans (Byzantines) and the Persians. Al-Bara fought to build a new world for them under the standard of Islam.

In one of the Iraqi wars, the Persians resorted to every means of barbarity. They used hooks fixed on the ends of heated chains and threw them from their castles to strike out at the Muslims. Al-Bara and his great brother Anas ibn Malik were assigned together with others to deal with one of these castles. But one of these hooks suddenly fell and caught Anas. He could not touch the chain to extricate himself as it was flaming hot.

When Al-Bara saw his brother being drawn up the castle wall on this hooked chain, he hurried to his aid. He grabbed the chain with his hands and bravely dismantled it. Anas was saved, but when Al-Bara took a look at his hands, he saw that all the flesh had been burnt away. The hero spent another long period in coalescence till he was fully healed.

The time for Al-Bara's death finally drew near. His moment came at the Battle of Tustur, where the Muslims met the Persian armies once more.

The people of Al-Ahwaz and Persia gathered together to form a large army to fight the Muslims. The Commander of the Faithful, Umar ibn

Al-Khattab, wrote to Sa'ad ibn Abu Waqas in Kufa and to Abu Musa Al-Ashari in Basra to each send an army to meet Al-Ahwaz. He told Abu Musa in his message, "Make Suhail ibn Adiy their leader and send Al-Bara ibn Malik with him." Thus, the Muslims gathered to face the enemy armies in a fierce battle. The two great brothers Anas ibn Malik and Al-Bara ibn Malik were among the believing soldiers.

The war began with duelling, and Al-Bara alone killed 100 of the Persian swordsmen. Then the armies joined the fray, and both sides suffered great losses. During the fight, some of the Companions came near Al-Bara and said, "Remember the Messenger's words about you, Bara: 'Perhaps there is a person with uncombed, dusty hair that people will not look at, but if he swears by Allah, He will fulfil his prayer. Among them is Al-Bara ibn Malik.' O Bara, swear by Allah, entreat Him to defeat them and render us victorious." Al-Bara immediately raised his palms towards the sky and supplicated, "O Allah, render them defeated and us victorious, and let me catch Your Prophet today." He took a long look at his brother Anas, who was fighting near him, as if saying farewell. Then the fighting intensified and the Muslims fought until they were victorious.

In answer to his prayer, Al-Bara was among the martyrs of the battle. His sword lay beside him, undamaged and his face looked content. Finally, the traveller had arrived at his home. Together with his martyred brothers, he ended the journey of a noble age.

(37)

UTBAH IBN GHAZWAN

Tomorrow You'll See the Nature of the Rulers after Me

Among the early Muslims, among the first Muhajirun, and among the extraordinary fighters of Islam was a towering, bright-faced, and humble-hearted man called Utbah ibn Ghazwan.

He was among the first seven people who embraced Islam by extending their right hands in pledge to the Messenger of Allah ﷺ. They pledged themselves to him while the Quraysh - with all their might and power for revenge – laid in wait, eager to persecute the new Muslims. In the first difficult days of the mission, Utbah ibn Ghazwan, together with his brothers, stood bravely against them.

When the Messenger of Allah ﷺ ordered his Companions to emigrate to Abyssinia, Utbah went with them, but his yearning for the Prophet did not allow him to settle there. Soon, he hurried back to Makkah where he stayed near the Messenger until it was time for the hijra to Medina. Then, Utbah emigrated again.

When the Quraysh began their provocations and wars against the Muslim, Utbah was always carrying his lance and bow, ready to use them expertly. He did not, however, put his weapons down after the noble Messenger died, but kept on fighting.

His jihad against the Persian armies was great. When Umar ibn Al-Khattab was Caliph, he sent him to conquer Al-Abullah to tackle the Persians there. They used it as a key military zone to combat the advancing Muslims who brought their message of Allah to His servants. When Umar was bidding Utbah and his army farewell, he said, "Proceed on your way until you reach the remotest Arab country and the nearest foreign country. Go, and may Allah bless you. Invite to Allah whoever answers you, and impose jizya (tax) upon whoever refuses or else use your sword without mercy. Wear the enemy down, and fear Allah your Lord."

Utbah advanced, heading his modest army until they reached Al-Abullah. There they faced the Persians, who were amassing one of their strongest armies. Utbah organised his troops and stood at the front, carrying his lance that never missed its target. He called out to his soldiers, "Allahu akbar (Allah is the Greatest), and Allah will fulfil His Promise". Al-Abullah surrendered whilst the Muslim army were still doing their patrols. Its land was purified of the Persian soldiers, and its people were liberated from the tyranny that had often tormented them. Almighty Allah had fulfilled His promise.

On the site of Al-Abullah, Utbah planned the city of Basra. He constructed it, and built its great mosque. When he wanted to leave the city and return to Medina, escaping from the responsibilities of rule, the Commander of the Faithful ordered him to stay. Utbah stayed in his place leading people in prayer, instructing them in religion, judging between them with justice, and giving them the most wonderful example in asceticism and piety. He fiercely fought the extravagance and luxury of those who liked comforts and desires.

One day he made a speech addressing them about worldly comforts. He said: "By Allah, I was the seventh of the first seven with the Messenger of Allah ﷺ, eating nothing but leaves of trees until the corners of our mouths were sore. I was given a garment. I cut it into two halves and gave one half to Sa'ad ibn Malik and I wore the other half."

Utbah used to fear the extravagance of the world, and in order to protect his religion and the Muslims from that, he tried to persuade them to practice asceticism and moderation. Many people tried to turn him from his way, to draw his attention to the allures and rights of authority. Such people used to respect the superficial appearance of high-ranking powers. But Utbah used to answer them saying: "I seek refuge in Allah from being great in your world and small in the sight of Allah." When he found people bored with his austerity, he induced them to be earnest saying, "Tomorrow you'll see the rulers after me."

When it was the Hajj season, he appointed one of his brothers as successor and went to perform the Hajj. When he finished, he travelled to Medina and asked the Commander of the Faithful to discharge him from the rule. But Umar would not lose the reverent ascetic who fled from what the mouths of mankind watered for. He used to say to them, "You burden me with your trusts and leave me alone? No, by Allah, I'll never discharge you." And that was what he said to Utbah ibn Ghazwan.

As Utbah could do nothing but obey, he took his camel and rode it back to Basra. But before he mounted it, he turned to the qibla and raised his imploring hands to heaven and invoked Almighty Allah not to return him to Basra or to government rule again. His invocation was answered, for while he was on his way to this rule, he died. His spirit was given up to its Creator. It was happy with the favour that Allah had completed upon it, and with the reward that Allah had prepared for it.

it back to Basra. But before he mounted it, he turned to the qibla and raised his imploring hands to heaven and invoked Almighty Allah not to return him to Basra or to govern that rule again. His invocation was answered, for while he was on his way to his rule, he died. His spirit was given up to its Creator. It was happy with the favour that Allah had completed upon it, and with the reward that Allah had prepared for it.

(38)

THABIT IBN QAIS

The Speaker for the Messenger of Allah

While Hassan was the poet of the Messenger of Allah ﷺ, Thabit was his speaker. The words he spoke were both eloquent, and perfectly comprehensive.

Thabit's skills were invaluable in the Year of Delegations, when some men from the Tamim tribe arrived in Medina. They said to the Messenger of Allah ﷺ, "We have come to brag, so please permit our poet and speaker [to speak]." The Messenger smiled and told them, "I permit your speaker. Let him speak." Their speaker, Utarid ibn Hajib, stood and boasted of his people's glories.

After he had finished, the Prophet ﷺ simply told Thabit ibn Qais, "Answer him." Thabit stood up and said, "All praise to Allah Who created the heavens and earth, in which He controls everything, Whose throne extends over the heavens and the earth. And nothing is at all except out of His kindness. It is part of His omnipotence to make us models and selected His Messenger out of the best of His creation, among whom he is of the noblest descent and the sincerest of speech. He sent him down His book and made His creation in trust of him. And he was the best choice of Allah. Then he called on people to believe in him. The Muhajirun of his people and his own kinsmen believed in him. They were of the noblest descent. Then we, the Ansar, were the first to respond. We are the adherents of Allah and the ministers of His Messenger." Such, was Thabit's eloquence.

Thabit witnessed the Battle of Uhud with the Messenger of Allah ﷺ and the battles that followed. He was always willing to sacrifice himself. In the apostasy wars, he used to be the vanguard, holding the Ansar's standard and striking out with a sword that never retreated. In the Battle of Yamama, Thabit witnessed the sudden assault that Musailamah launched against the Muslims at the start of the battle. Thabit shouted in a loud, warning voice, "By Allah, we did not use to fight that way with the Messenger of Allah ﷺ!" Then he went away, and returned only after anointing himself and putting on his burial shroud. He shouted once more, "O Allah! I clear myself of what those people have done (i.e. the army of Musailamah) and I apologise to You for what they have done (i.e. the Muslims' slackness in fighting)."

Then the Prophet's servant, Salim, who was holding the standard of the Muhajirun, joined Thabit. They both dug a deep hole for themselves and stood in it. They piled up the sand around them till it covered their hips. They stood as if two rooted mountains, with their lower halves fixedly buried in the sand, and their upper bodies took on the armies of paganism.

They struck out with their swords at Musailamah's army until they were both martyred in their place. The sight of them alone (may Allah be pleased with them) brought many Muslims back to their positions and they fought the Musailamah the Liar's army into to the trodden sand.

Thabit ibn Qais, who excelled in his life as both a speaker and warrior, used to be self-reproaching and strive to humble himself to Allah. Among the Muslims, he was extremely modest and afraid of Allah.

When this noble verse was sent down: *God does not love any proud and boastful one* (31:18), Thabit shut his house door and kept crying. It was a long time before the Messenger of Allah ﷺ heard about this. When he did, he sent for him and asked him the reason. Thabit said, "O Messenger of Allah! I like beautiful clothes and footwear. I am afraid to be of the arrogant." The Prophet ﷺ laughed contentedly and answered, "You are not one of them. You'll live and die with blessings and enter Paradise."

And when the following words of Allah the Exalted were sent down: *O you who believe! Don't raise your voices above the Prophet's voice, and do not speak loudly to him, as you speak to one another, lest your deeds are rendered fruitless, while you are unaware* (49:2), Thabit shut himself indoors again and kept crying. When the Messenger missed him, he enquired about and sent for him. When Thabit came, the Prophet ﷺ asked him the reason for his absence. Thabit answered, "I have a loud voice and I used to raise my voice above your voice, Messenger of Allah ﷺ. My deeds are rendered fruitless then, and I'm of the people of the Fire." The Messenger of Allah answered reassuringly, "You are not one of them. You'll live praiseworthily and be martyred, and Allah will let you into Paradise."

One incident is left in Thabit's story. Those who are focused on the tangible and materialistic in this world might not feel comfortable with this narration. In spite of this, the incident is quite easily explained.

After Thabit had fallen martyr in battle, one of the newer Muslims passed by him and saw Thabit's precious armour on his corpse. He thought it was his right to take it and he did.

Elsewhere, a Muslim man was sleeping. Suddenly, Thabit appeared to him in a dream and said to him, "I entrust you with my will, so be careful not to say it's a dream and waste it. When I fell martyr yesterday, a Muslim man passed by me and took my armour. His house is on the outskirts of the town. His horse is tall. He put his pot on the armour and above the pot put his saddle. Go to Khalid and tell him to take it. And when you go to Medina and meet the successor of the Messenger of Allah ﷺ, Abu Bakr, tell him I owe so-and-so. Let him pay my loan."

When the man woke up, he went to Khalid ibn Al-Walid and related his dream to him. Khalid sent someone to retrieve the armour, and he found it exactly as Thabit had described it in that dream. When the Muslims went back to Medina, the Muslim man narrated the dream to the Caliph, and he too fulfilled Thabit's will. There is not in Islam a dead man's will that was fulfilled in such a way after his death, except that of Thabit ibn Qais.

Truly, man is a big mystery! *Think not of those who are killed in the Way of Allah as dead. Nay, they are alive, with their Lord, and they have provision.* (3:169).

(39)

USAID IBN HUDAIR

The Hero of the Day of As-Saqifah

Usaid inherited his noble characteristics as handed down from father to son. His father, Hudair Al-Kata'ib, was a leader of the Al-Aws tribe, and a strong Arab fighter from the pre-Islamic era. From his father, Usaid inherited his status, his courage, and his hospitality.

Before becoming Muslim, Usaid was one of Medina's leaders, a noble amongst the Arabs, and one of their most excellent spearmen. When Usaid was attracted to Islam and guided to the way of the Almighty, he was then best honoured as one of Allah's Ansar.

He embraced Islam quickly, decisively, and honourably. It all began when the Messenger ﷺ sent Musab ibn Umair to Medina. He was tasked with teaching the Muslim Ansar there more about Islam (after their Pledge at Aqabah), and calling others to Allah's religion.

On Musab's arrival, local leaders Usaid ibn Hudair and Sa'ad ibn Muad were discussing this stranger who had come from Makkah to denounce their religion and call them to a new, unknown one. Sa'ad said to Usaid, "Go directly to this man and deter him." So, Usaid carried his spear and hurried to Musab. He went to see Musab at Asad ibn Zurarah's house, one of the Medinan leaders who was among the early believers in Islam.

There, where Musab and Asad Ibn Zurarah were sitting, Usaid saw a crowd of people listening carefully to Musab as he called them to Allah. Usaid surprised them with an angry outburst. Musab said to him, "Won't you sit down and listen? If our matter pleases you, accept it, and if you hate it, we'll stop calling you to what you hate."

Usaid was an enlightened and intelligent man whom the people of Medina called 'Al Kamil' (The Perfect), a nickname that his father used to bear before him. So, when he found Musab appealing to logic and reason, he stuck his spear in the ground and said to him, "You're right, tell me what you have."

Musab started reciting the Holy Quran to him and explaining to him the call of the new, true religion. Those who attended this assembly said, "By Allah, we saw Islam in Usaid's face before he spoke. We knew it because of his brilliance and easiness." No sooner did Musab finish his words than Usaid was overwhelmed by them and shouted, "How good these words are! What do you do if you want to embrace this religion?" Musab said, "Purify your body and clothes, and bear true witness, then pray."

Usaid's character was straight, strong, and clear. He would not hesitate a second in face of strong opposition, if he knew his own way. So, Usaid got up quickly to welcome the new faith, which was already penetrating his heart and overwhelming his soul. He purified himself, prostrated to Allah in worship, and immediately announced his embracement of Islam and abandonment of paganism.

Usaid had to return to Sa'ad ibn Muad to give him the news of his encounter with Musab. As he approached, Sa'ad said to those around him, "Usaid's face is changed. I swear it." He went with a challenging, angry face and came back with a face full of mercy and light.

Usaid decided to use his intelligence. He knew that Sa'ad ibn Muad was well known for his pure nature and keen determination. He knew that Islam would not be far from him. He only needed to hear what he himself had heard of Allah's word, which the Messenger's envoy to them, Musab ibn Umair, was expert at reciting and explaining. But, if he said to Sa'ad, "I've embraced Islam; go and embrace it", the outcome would not have been ensured. He had to prompt Sa'ad in a way that would push him to Musab's gathering, in order to observe and listen himself. How could he do this?

As we said before, Musab was a guest at Asad ibn Zurarah's house. Asad was Sa'ad ibn Muad's cousin. So, Usaid said to Sa'ad, "I was told that the Haritha tribe went out to kill Asad ibn Zurarah and they know he is your cousin."

Angry and heated, Sa'ad took his spear and ran fast to where Musab and the Muslims were sitting. When he came near the gathering, he found nothing but a great quiet overwhelming them. Musab ibn Umair sat in the middle of the group, reciting Allah's verses humbly, and they all carefully listened to him.

Just then, he realised the trick that Usaid had played on him to make him go to this gathering and listen to what the envoy of Islam was saying. So, Usaid's insight into his friend's character proved to be accurate. But, Sa'ad had hardly heard the Quran when Allah opened his heart to Islam, and soon he took his place among the early believers.

Usaid bore a strong, bright belief in his heart and mind. His belief filled him with patience and discernment, that all made him a trustworthy man.

During the expedition against Banu Al-Mustaliq, the hypocrisy of a man called Abdullah ibn Ubaiy became apparent. In anger after the battle, he spoke of the Prophet and his Companions to the Medinan people around him: "You've let them enter your town and share your money. By Allah, if you cease giving them what you have, they'll turn to another place. By Allah, if we return to Medina, indeed the more honourable will expel the meaner from there."

The venerable Companion, Zaid ibn Arqam heard these poisoned hypocritical words from someone who claimed to be a Muslim. So, he had to inform the Messenger of Allah ﷺ. The Messenger was much hurt. When he met Usaid he said, "Don't you know what your friend has said?" Usaid asked, "Which friend, O Messenger of Allah?" The Messenger of Allah answered, "Abdullah ibn Ubaiy." Usaid asked, "What did he say?" The Messenger said, "He claimed that if he returned to Medina, the more honourable will expel the meaner from there." Then Usaid said, "By Allah, *you*, O Messenger of Allah, will expel him from there, by Allah's permission. By Allah, he is the meaner and you are the more honourable."

He added, "O Messenger of Allah, treat him gently. By Allah, Allah brought you to us while the people of Abdullah were preparing to crown him king of Medina. He sees that Islam has deprived him of kingship." With this calm, profound thinking, Usaid used to solve problems using his presence of mind.

On another occasion, on the Day of As-Saqifah (soon after the death of the Messenger of Allah ﷺ), a group of the Ansar, headed by Sa'ad ibn Ubadah, announced their right to succession and sparked a furious debate. Usaid, who as we know was a prominent member of the Ansar, took a calm and positive attitude to settle the matter. He stood to address the group of Ansar saying, "You know that the Messenger of Allah ﷺ was one of the Muhajirun. His successor, then, should be one of the Muhajirun. We used to be the Ansar of the Messenger of Allah. Today we have to be the Ansar of his successor." His words brought about calm, peace and security.

Usaid ibn Hudair (may Allah be pleased with him) spent his life as a humble worshipper, sacrificing his energy and money in the cause of goodness. He often reminded himself of the Prophet's ﷺ advice to the Ansar: "Be patient until you meet me in the realm of Paradise."

Usaid was held in high esteem by Abu Bakr Al-Siddiq because of his religiosity and noble manners. He also had the same status in Umar's heart, and indeed in the hearts of all the Companions. Listening to his voice while reciting Quran was one of the greatest honours that the Companions aspired to. His voice was so humble and resonant that the Messenger ﷺ once said the angels came near him one night, just to hear it.

In the month of Shaban 20 AH, Usaid died. The Commander of the Faithful, Umar, insisted on carrying his bier on his shoulders. Under the earth of Al-Baqi, the Companions buried the body of a great believer. They went back to Medina remembering his virtues and repeating the noble Messenger's words about him: "What an excellent man Usaid ibn Hudair is!"

(40)

ABDUR RAHMAN IBN AWF

Blessed in Pursuit of the Halal

One calm day in Medina, heavy dust began accumulating in the air till it nearly covered the horizon. People thought it was a raging storm, but soon beyond the dust, they heard the noise of a great caravan. After a while, 700 heavily laden camels were crowding the streets. People called to each other to rejoice at the provisions the caravan might be carrying.

The Mother of the Faithful, Aisha (may Allah be pleased with her), heard about the coming caravan and asked, "What's going on in Medina?" She was answered, "It's a caravan of Abdur Rahman ibn Awf coming from Syria carrying his goods." Aisha said, "But can one caravan make all this tremor?" "Yes, Mother of the Faithful. There are 700 camels." Aisha nodded and looked away as if searching her memory, then she said suddenly, "I heard the Messenger of Allah ﷺ saying (once), 'I saw Abdur Rahman ibn Awf crawling into Paradise'." Indeed, this was his caravan.

But, why would Ibn Awf not hurry into Paradise? When some of Ibn Awf's friends informed him of what Aisha had said, he too remembered that he had also heard the Prophet ﷺ say that hadith more than once. Therefore, before unloading the camels, he hastened to Aisha's house and told her, "I call you to witness that this caravan with all its loads is in the cause of Allah Almighty." And the loads of 700 camels were distributed among the people of Medina and the places around it in a great festival of charity. It was in response to this hadith that Ibn Awf had always hastened towards charitable giving, in the hope of untying the burden of his wealth.

This incident alone represents the true image of Abdur Rahman ibn Awf's life. He was a very successful merchant and a rich man. He was also a wise believer, who refused that his portion of this life would ever sweep away his religion; or that his fortune would make him lag behind the caravan of belief, denying him the reward of Paradise. He (may Allah be pleased with him) would rather generously sacrifice his fortune and feel satisfied.

When and how did this great man embrace Islam? He did so very early in the first hours of the mission. He even did so before the Messenger of Allah ﷺ entered Dar Al-Arqam's house to meet his other faithful

Companions. He was one of the first eight believers in Islam. From the time he embraced Islam till he died at the age of 75, he was a splendid model of a great believer. The Prophet counted him among the ten to whom he gave glad tidings of inheriting Paradise. This also made Umar (may Allah be pleased with him) count him among the six advisers to whom he assigned succession after himself. He said, "The Messenger of Allah ﷺ died while pleased with them."

After Abdur Rahman embraced Islam, he faced his own portion of the persecution and challenges from the Quraysh. When the Prophet ﷺ ordered his Companions to emigrate to Abyssinia, Ibn Awf emigrated but soon returned to Makkah. Then, he emigrated to Abyssinia again in the second migration. From there he settled in Medina, where he fought in Badr, Uhud, and all the other battles.

He was very lucky in his trade to such an extent that even he was amazed. He said, "If I lift up a stone, I find silver and gold under it." Trade for Abdur Rahman ibn Awf was not for greed or monopoly. It was not even to satisfy a hunger for riches. It was simply a duty to work. His success just made him enjoy that work more, and encouraged him to exert more effort in its pursuit. He had an enthusiastic nature, so he found comfort in any honourable work, whatever it was. If he was not praying in the mosque or fighting a battle, he was working in his trade. That trade thrived so much that his caravans arrived in Medina from Egypt and Syria, laden with everything that the Arabian peninsula might need in both garments and food.

After the Muslims' hijra to Medina, his ebullient nature was clear to all. In those days the Messenger ﷺ paired off every two of his Companions as brothers: a Muhajir (emigrant) from Makkah with an Ansar (helper) from Medina. This association was both unique and effective in every way. Each of the Ansar in Medina shared everything that he owned with his Muhajir brother.

The noble Messenger ﷺ joined Abdur Rahman ibn Awf and Sa'ad ibn Ar-Rabuiah as brothers one day. Let us listen to the noble Companion Anas ibn Malik (may Allah be pleased with him) narrating what happened:

"Sa'ad said to Abdur Rahman, 'O brother, I'm the richest in Medina. Take half of my fortune. And I have two wives. Choose the one you like better and I'll divorce her for you to marry.' So Abdur Rahman ibn

Awf said, 'Allah bless your family and money. (Just) show me the way to the market.' He went to the market, bought, sold, and gained profit."

That is how he led his life in Medina, whether during the Messenger's lifetime or after his death. What made his trade blessed and successful was his pursuit of the halal, and his strict avoidance of the haram, or even the doubtful. What made it even more blessed and successful was that it was not for Abdur Rahman alone. Allah had a bigger share in it, by which he used to strengthen the ties of his family and brothers and prepare the armies of Islam. If commerce and fortune are usually evaluated on the basis of stocks on hand and profits, Abdur Rahman ibn Awf's fortune was evaluated on the basis of what was spent from it in the cause of Allah, the Lord of All the Worlds.

One day, he heard the Messenger of Allah ﷺ saying to him, "O Ibn Awf, you are a rich man, and you are going to crawl into Paradise. So, lend to Allah in order to set your feet free." Ever since he heard this advice from the Messenger of Allah, he started lending to Allah a goodly loan. Then Allah increased it manifold to His credit in repaying.

One day, he sold some land for 40,000 dinars and distributed it all to the people of the Zuhrah tribe, the Mothers of the Faithful, and the poor Muslims. The next day, he provided the Islamic armies with 500 horses, and on the third day with 1,500 camels.

When he was about to die, he bequeathed 5,000 dinars in the cause of Allah, and 400 dinars to each person who was still living who had fought in Badr. Even Uthman ibn Affan (may Allah be pleased with him) took his share of the gift in spite of his riches and said, "Abdur Rahman's money is halal and pure. Its food gives health and blessing."

Ibn Awf was the master of his money, not its slave. The proof of this was that he did not have trouble gathering halal money. And, he did not enjoy it alone, but always together with his family, brethren, and all his community. He was so generous and hospitable that he used to say, "The people of Medina are partners of Ibn Awf in his money. He lends to a third of them, pays the debts of a third, and strengthens his ties of kinship by giving away a third."

These riches would not have made him happy if they stopped him from adhering to his religion and supporting his brethren. Nevertheless, he was always apprehensive of these riches. One day when he was fasting, he was served iftar (the meal at sunset which breaks the fast). He had hardly seen it when he lost his appetite and cried saying, "When Musab ibn Umair was martyred - and he was better than me - he was wrapped in his garment so that if it covered his head, his feet showed, and if it covered his feet, his head showed. When Hamza was martyred - and he was better than me - they found nothing to wrap him with except his garment. Now the world has been expanded for us, and we have been given much. I'm afraid our blessings are hastened."

Another day, some of his friends gathered around food in his home. Just as it was put in front of them, he wept. They asked him, "What makes you weep, O Abu Muhammad?" He answered, "The Messenger of Allah ﷺ died when he and his family had not even satisfied their appetites with barley bread. I can't see that our latter days have shown something better."

In addition, his large fortune never brought out pride in him, so much so that they said of him, "If a stranger sees him sitting among his servants, he wouldn't be able to distinguish him from the others." If only this stranger would know even a fraction of Ibn Awf's fortitude and good deeds, he would recognise his worth instantly in the eyes of Allah. That, for example, he suffered 20 wound at the Battle of Uhud, one of which left a permanent lameness in one leg. And that some of his teeth fell out on that same day, leaving a clear defect in his articulation. This tall and bright faced man never showed an ounce of pride, but was worthy of much praise.

When Umar ibn Al-Khattab (may Allah be pleased with him) was dying, he chose six Companions of the Messenger of Allah ﷺ to select from among themselves the new successor. All fingers pointed at Ibn Awf. Some Companions even conversed with him about his right to win succession, but he said, "By Allah, it is better for me to put a knife in my throat and penetrate it to the other side."

Thus, the six chosen Companions had hardly held a meeting to select one of them to succeed Umar 'Al-Faruq' (The One Who Distinguishes Truth from Falsehood), when Ibn Awf informed them that he was renouncing the right given to him by Umar. Soon, this ascetic attitude made him the judge of the other, noble five men. They agreed that he would select the successor among them. Imam Ali said, "I heard the Messenger of Allah ﷺ describing you as honest among the people of heaven and earth." Finally, Ibn Awf selected Uthman ibn Affan successor, and all the rest agreed with him.

Although he was a truly rich man, it was Islam that put him above his riches, and moulded him in the best fashion. In 32 AH Ibn Awf's soul ascended to its Creator. Aisha, the Mother of the Faithful, wanted to bestow a special honour on him. As he was in the death throes, she proposed that when he passed they should bury him near the Messenger ﷺ, Abu Bakr, and Umar. But, as a Muslim he was too modest to put himself in that rank. Besides, he had made a previous promise. One day, he and Uthman ibn Madhun had promised each other that whoever died after the other would be buried near his friend.

While his soul was preparing for its new journey, his eyes were dripping with tears and his tongue was stammering, "I am afraid of being held up by my friends because of what I had of abundant money." But soon, calmness overwhelmed him, and a tender happiness covered his face. His ears listened closely, as if there were a sweet voice coming near them. Perhaps he was listening then to the truth of the Messenger's words ﷺ to him, "Abdur Rahman ibn Awf will enter Paradise." And, maybe he was also listening to Allah's promise in His book: *Those Who spend their wealth in Cause of Allah, and do not follow up their gifts with reminders of their generosity or with injury, their reward is with their Lord. On them shall be no fear, nor shall they grieve.* (2:261-262)

(41)

‘ABU JABIR’ ABDULLAH IBN AMR IBN HIRAM

Shaded by Angels

When 70 men of the Ansar swore their allegiance to Prophet Muhammad ﷺ in the Second Pledge of Aqabah, Abdullah ibn Amr ibn Hiram was amongst them. And, when the Prophet chose some leaders from those 70, Abdullah ibn Amr was one of these leaders. The Prophet made him the leader of his people, the Banu Salamah. When they returned to Medina, he sacrificed himself, his money, and his family to the service of Islam. And, after the Prophet's hijra to Medina, Abu Jabir (as he was known) found utmost enjoyment in accompanying the Prophet ﷺ day and night.

In the Battle of Badr, he went out fighting like a hero. At Uhud he dreamt of his death before the Muslims went out to battle. He was overwhelmed by a true sense that he was not coming back, but his heart was full of joy. He called his son, the noble Companion Jabir ibn Abdullah, and said to him, "I see myself killed in this battle. Maybe I'll be the first martyr among the Muslims. By Allah, I'll leave no one that I like more than you after the Messenger of Allah ﷺ. I am in debt, so pay my debts and make your brothers your own concern."

The next morning the Muslims went out to encounter the Quraysh that had come to invade their peaceful city. A dreadful battle raged, and the Muslims achieved a quick victory at the start. It could have been decisive, but for the archers. As aforementioned, the Messenger ﷺ had ordered that they stay in their positions regardless, but they were tempted by their victory over the Quraysh. They left their positions on the mountain and were preoccupied with gathering the booty of the defeated army. Meanwhile, the Quraysh quickly gathered themselves when they found the Muslims' back flank completely exposed. They formed a surprised attack that soon changed the Muslim victory into a defeat.

It was during this bitter fight that Abdullah ibn Amr died as a martyr. When the Muslims went to find their martyrs after the battle, Jabir ibn Abdullah went to search for his father. He found him among the martyrs, whom the polytheists had made a dreadful display of along with other war heroes. Jabir and his family were crying over their father, Abdullah ibn Amr, when the Messenger of Allah ﷺ passed by. He said, "Cry over him or not, the angels are here to shade him with their wings!"

Abu Jabir's belief had been strong. His desire to die for the cause of Allah was his greatest ambition. After the Prophet had announced the high regard for martyrdom in Islam, Abdullah had always shared a fondness for the prospect. One day, the Prophet ﷺ found Abdullah's son sad. Jabir narrates:

"The Messenger of Allah looked at me one day and said, 'O Jabir, why do I see you sad?' I said, 'O Messenger of Allah! My father was martyred and left behind debts and children.' He said 'Should I tell you that Allah never spoke to anyone except from behind a veil, however He spoke to your father directly. He said `Ask Me and I will give you.' He said, 'O Allah, I ask You to return me to earth, to be killed again in Your cause'. The Lord, Exalted be He said, 'I have said before: They shall not return back to it [this life].' Then, he said, 'O Lord, then convey the news to those I left behind.' So Allah revealed: *Think not of those who are killed in the way of Allah as dead Nay, they are alive, with their Lord, and they have provision. They rejoice in what Allah has bestowed upon them of His Bounty, rejoicing for the sake of those who have not joined them, but are left behind (not yet martyred) that on them no fear shall come, nor shall they grieve.*" (3:169-170).

When the Muslims were identifying their pious martyrs after the Battle of Uhud and the family of Abdullah ibn Amr had identified his corpse, his wife carried him, together with her brother who was martyred also, on her camel. She began taking them back to Medina to bury them there. Likewise did some other Muslims for their martyrs. But the crier of the Messenger of Allah ﷺ caught up with them and announced the Messenger's order: Bury the martyrs on their battle-ground. So, they all returned with their martyrs.

The noble Prophet ﷺ was supervising the burial of his martyred Companions who had sacrificed their precious souls as humble offerings to Allah and His Messenger. When it was Abdullah ibn Amr's turn to be buried, the Messenger of Allah ﷺ called, "Bury Abdullah ibn Amr and Amr ibn Al-Jamuuh in one grave; they were loving and sincere to each other in this world."

Now, during the moments of preparing the happy grave to receive the two noble martyrs, let us have a loving look at the second martyr, Amr Ibn Al-Jamuuh.

(42)

AMR IBN AL-JAMUUH

Walking Proudly in Paradise

Amr was related to Abdullah ibn Amr ibn Hiram by marriage, being the husband of his sister, Hind bint Amr. Amr ibn Al-Jamuuh was one of the leaders of Medina and a chief of the Salamah tribe. His son, Mifadh ibn Amr, was one of the 70 Ansar at the pledge of Aqabah and preceded him in his Islam.

Muad ibn Amr and his friend Muad ibn Jabal were calling the people of Medina to Islam with the enthusiasm characteristic of bold youth. It was a custom that the nobles kept symbolic idols as figurines in their houses. As a nobleman and chief, Amr ibn Al-Jamuuh made an idol to install in his house, and called it Manaf. His son, Muad ibn Amr, agreed with his comrade Muad ibn Jabal to make his father's idol an object of ridicule.

They used to enter his house at night, take the idol and throw it into a cesspit. And when Amr would wake up he would not find Manaf in its place, and would keep looking for it till he found it thrown into that pit. He used to fly into a rage and say, "Woe unto you, who transgressed our gods this night!" Then he would wash and perfume it. When night came again, the 'two Muads', would do to the idol as they had done the previous night.

When Amr got weary he took his sword and put it to Manaf's neck and said to it, "If you are a beneficial god defend yourself." When he woke up though, he still did not find the idol in its place, but discarded again in the same cesspit. This time, it was not in the pit alone, but tied to a dead dog by a strong rope.

While he was angry and surprised, some of the already Muslim nobles of Medina approached him. They pointed at the ridiculed idol and appealed Amr ibn Al-Jamuuh's good sense. They spoke to him about the Most True and Most High, Allah, Whom there is nothing like. They talked to him about the trustworthy, faithful Muhammad who came to give, not to take; to guide, not to misguide. They talked to him about Islam that came to liberate mankind from all the shackles, revive the spirit of Allah in them, and spread His light in their hearts.

In a few moments, Amr discovered himself and his destiny. He purified and perfumed his clothes and body. Then he went, with his head high, to acknowledge the Seal of the Prophets ﷺ and to take his place among the believers.

One might wonder how those nobles and leaders, like Amr ibn Al-Jamuuh, could believe in helpless idols to that extent in the first place. How did their reason not restrain them? In the past, however, people's hearts used to embrace such actions. Their intelligence was helpless against the strong sense of tradition.

For example, in the days of Pericles, Pythagoras, and Socrates, Athens was famed for its intellectual progress. However, its people - including philosophers and judges - used to believe in man-made idols. Quite simply, religious progress in those times was not as developed as intellectual progress. It is of course, the nature of man to rely on such physical concepts of deity; and that is why even in this modern age of information, we see a reliance on such idols to this day.

Amr ibn Al-Jamuuh dedicated his heart and life to Allah. Although he was generous by nature, Islam made him even more generous. So much so that he put all his money in to the service of his religion and his brethren.

The Messenger ﷺ asked a group from the Banu Salamah (the tribe of Amr ibn Al-Jamuuh), "Who is your chief, O Banu Salamah?" They answered, "Al-Jad ibn Qais, in spite of his being a miser." He ﷺ said, "No, your chief is the white curly haired Amr ibn Al-Jamuuh" This testimony from the Messenger of Allah was a great honour to Ibn Al-Jamuuh.

Just as Amr dedicated his money in the cause of Allah, so too was he willing to sacrifice his life, but how? There was a severe lameness in his leg that made him unable to participate in battle. He had four sons who were all strong Muslim men. They used to go out with the Messenger ﷺ in his expeditions, and fulfilled their duty to defend Islam. Amr had tried to join the Battle of Badr. His sons though implored the Prophet to persuade him not to go out, or even to order him to stay if he was not persuaded. So, the Prophet ﷺ told him that Islam exempted him from jihad because of his disability. When he began pleading, the Prophet ordered him to stay in Medina.

Then the Battle of Uhud came, and Amr went to the Prophet again, imploring him to permit his participation. He said, "O Messenger of Allah, my sons want to prevent me from going out with you to fight. By Allah, I want to walk proudly with my lameness in Paradise." Since he pleaded his case so well, the Prophet ﷺ permitted him to go out So, he took his weapon and set out to walk happily, invoking Allah in a submissive voice, "O Allah, bestow martyrdom upon me and don't return me to my family."

When the two rival forces met on the Day of Uhud, Amr ibn Al-Jamuuh and his four sons set out together to fight the polytheists. Amr walked proudly amidst the fierce battle and his sword struck out with precision at his enemy. He looked to the horizon as he fought, as if hastening the arrival of the angel of death.

He asked his Lord for martyrdom, certain that Allah would respond to him. That which he had been waiting for, finally happened. The blow of a sword announced the time of his martyrdom.

As we know, when the Muslims were burying their martyrs, the Messenger ﷺ repeated his order: "Put Abdullah ibn Amr ibn Hiram and Amr ibn Al-Jamuuh in one grave; they were loving and sincere to each other in this world." The two loving friends and martyrs were buried in one grave under the very battlefield that witnessed their extraordinary bravery.

Forty-six years after they and their companions had been buried, a fountain head of water (made by Muawiyah) erupted and a violent torrent of water covered that same graveyard. The Muslims hurried to remove the martyrs' bodies. They were surprised, however, to find them as, "Having soft bodies and flexible limbs."

Abdullah's son, Jabir, was still alive and so he went with his family to remove the bodies of his father, Abdullah ibn Amr ibn Hiram, and his aunt's husband, Amr ibn Al-Jamuuh. However, he found them in their grave as if they were sleeping. They were not changed at all. We needn't be surprised by this narration. The pious and pure of soul are known to leave their bodies intact, with a kind of immunity from the influence of the soil. Such is their status even in the next life.

(43)

HABIB IBN ZAID

A Legend of Sacrifice and Love

Among those blessed men and women who swore faithfulness to the Prophet at the Second Pledge of Aqabah, were Habib ibn Zaid and his father Zaid ibn Asim (may Allah be pleased with both of them). Habib's mother was Nusaybah bint Kab, one of the two women who were the first to swear allegiance there. The second woman was Habib's maternal aunt. Thus, he was a believer, whose faith ran in his blood. He lived near the Prophet ﷺ after he emigrated to Medina. And once there, he never missed an expedition or opportunity in the cause of Allah.

Once, in the south of the Arab Peninsula there emerged two arrogant individuals who claimed false prophethood and tried to drag others into their swamp of disbelief. One of these impostors was called Al-Aswad ibn Kab Al Ansiy, from Sana. The other was Musailamah the Liar from Yamama. Both impostors incited people against the believers in their tribes, believers who responded to what Allah ordained and who believed in the Last Prophet ﷺ. They also goaded them against the Prophet's messengers sent to their lands. Moreover, they even went so far as to ignite suspicion against the prophethood itself and committed mischief in the land, that spread corruption.

One day, the Prophet ﷺ was surprised when a messenger arrived with a message from Musailamah in which he said, "From Musailamah, Allah's Prophet to Muhammad, Allah's Prophet. Peace be upon you. We are your partner in prophethood; consequently, we have half of the earth and the Quraysh has the other half, but the Quraysh want unjustly to have it all!"

The Prophet ﷺ summoned one of his scribes and dictated this answer to Musailamah: "In the name of Allah, the Most Beneficent, the Most Merciful. From Muhammad, the Prophet of Allah, to Musailamah the Liar. Peace be upon those who followed the right path. Verily, the earth is Allah's. He gives it as a heritage to whom He will of His slaves and the blessed end is for the pious and righteous persons who fear Allah."

The Prophet's words were direct and clear. They exposed the liar of Banu Hanifah. Musailamah thought that prophethood was a kingdom, and so he demanded his piece of the cake, or as he put it, "half the earth and its people". The messenger carried the Prophet's answer to Musailamah, but it only made him more mischievous and corrupt.

He went on spreading his falsehood and abusing the believers in his midst by instigating people against them. The Prophet ﷺ thought it best to give him one last chance, so he sent a message to convince him not to commit any more of his folly. He picked Habib ibn Zaid as his messenger. Habib enthusiastically set out on the mission that the Prophet had entrusted him with. He hoped that Musailamah's heart would be guided to the right path and that he would be rewarded in the Hereafter.

The traveller reached his destination. Musailamah the Liar read the Prophet's message, but he was blinded by its light, which only made him more arrogant. He lacked the sense of honour and decency of the Arabs, which might have otherwise prevented him from shedding the blood of a messenger, which was highly respected and even held sacred by all Arabs. On that day, Islam offered humanity a new lesson in heroism. Only this time, both its subject matter and its tutor were one and the same person: Habib ibn Zaid.

Musailamah the Liar called upon his people to witness one of his 'memorable' events. The Prophet's messenger, Habib ibn Zaid, was brought in. It was clear from his wounds that he had been abused and severely tortured by his captors. They thought that they could strip him of his valour by humiliating him before the crowd. They hoped that he would then give Musailamah the credibility he craved, when he called upon him to witness to his fake prophethood before them. In doing so, the notorious liar would be able to perform a fake miracle to cement his prestige among those he had already deluded.

Therefore, Musailamah asked Habib, "Do you bear witness that Muhammad is, indeed, the Messenger of Allah?" Habib answered boldly, "Yes, I do bear witness that Muhammad is, indeed, the Messenger of Allah." Musailamah's face went white with humiliation and embarrassment yet he asked, "Do you bear witness that I am the Messenger of Allah?" Habib scornfully replied, "Nonsense!"

The impostor Musailamah's face darkened with rage. His scheme had failed. Habib's torture had been futile. Habib was slapped fiercely before the crowd, gathered to witness Musailamah's so-called miracle. This slap was so aggressive that it shattered the image of his assumed dignity. He became violent and summoned his executioner, who hurriedly stabbed Habib's body with his sword. The executioner cruelly cut Habib to pieces, and whilst he still could, Habib chanted stoically, "There is no god but Allah and Muhammad is His Messenger."

If on that day Habib had tried to escape this horrible death by pretending he believed in Musailamah's prophethood, because of the circumstances Habib's Islam would not have been blemished in any way. But, he was a man who could not for a moment hold his life and principles as separable. He had pledged his loyalty to the Prophet with his family some time before. Therefore, he found a rare opportunity to prove the meaning of his life once and for all. His life was an embodiment of his faith. It embodied his steadfastness, heroism, sacrifice, and martyrdom for the sake of honour and truth, the splendour of which surpassed all victories.

The Prophet received the sad news of Habib's martyrdom with patience, for Allah's inspiration made him see the future fate of Musailamah. He could almost see his death with his own eyes. As for Nusaybah bint Kab, Habib's mother, she gnashed her teeth for a long while on hearing the terrible deed. But, then she swore a solemn oath to avenge her son's death upon Musailamah and to thrust her sword and spear right into his wicked body. Fate must have watched her anguish, patience, and courage on receiving this news. It must have had sympathy for her calamity, as fate stood by Nusaybah until she fulfilled her oath.

After a short while, the Battle of Yamama took place. Abu Bakr Al-Siddiq, the Prophet's Caliph, organised an army to march to Yamama where Musailamah had already organised a huge army. Nusaybah marched along with the Muslim army and threw herself into the battlefield, armed with a sword in her right hand and a spear in her left one. She kept on shouting, "Where are you Musailamah, you enemy of Allah?"

When Musailamah was killed and his followers dissipated like carded wool, the standards of Islam fluttered in victory. Nusaybah's strong and brave body was strained with spear wounds. She stood there recalling the amiable face of her beloved son that seemed to linger nearby. Wherever she looked, she saw the face of her son Habib. It was somewhere out there, smiling contentedly on every victorious flag.

(44)

UBAIY IBN KAB

Rejoice with the Knowledge, Abu Al-Mundhir

The Prophet ﷺ asked Abu Al-Mundhir one day, "Which is the greatest verse in the Holy Quran?" He answered, "Allah and His Prophet know best." The Prophet ﷺ then repeated his question, "Which is the greatest verse in the Holy Quran, Abu Al- Mundhir?" Ubaiy finally answered, "*Allah! None has the right to be worshiped but He, the Ever-Living, the One Who Sustains and protects all that exists...*" (2:255) The Prophet's face brightened with joy as he patted Abu Al-Mundhir on the back and said, "I congratulate you for having such knowledge and insight, Abu Al-Mundhir."

Abu Al-Mundhir was also known as Ubaiy ibn Kab, the great Companion. He was one of the Ansar of Medina, who helped and aided the Muhajirun. He belonged to the Al-Khazraj tribe. He witnessed the Pledge of Aqabah, the Battle of Badr, and was part of all the main events of Islam. He held a highly distinguished position among those who were the first to commit themselves to Islam. Umar, the Commander of the Faithful, once said, "Ubaiy is the master of the Muslims."

Ubaiy ibn Kab was one of the first Muslim scribes who wrote down the revelation that descended on the Prophet ﷺ, as well as his messages. He was a pioneer in learning the Holy Quran by heart, and recited it in a slow, pleasant tone to comprehend its content.

One day, the Prophet ﷺ said to Ubaiy, "I was ordered to recite the Quran to you." Ubaiy was overwhelmed and asked the Prophet anxiously, "You are dearer to me than my own mother and father! Please tell me, did the Spirit mention me by name?" The Prophet ﷺ answered, "Yes, it resounded your very name and your family name in the kingdom of heaven and earth."

Now, a Muslim who was so close to the Prophet ﷺ must indeed be a special one. Throughout the years in which Ubaiy accompanied the Prophet, he tried to stay close to him so as to quench his thirst for Islam from the Prophet's inexhaustible spring. Ubaiy ibn Kab adhered tenaciously to his covenant in worship, piety, and conduct. Even after the Prophet's death, he was always there to warn people against wrongdoing and remind them of their pledge, morals, and asceticism from the times when the Prophet was alive. He was known to say to his companions, "We stood as one man when the Prophet was alive, but as soon as he departed we went in different directions."

Ubaiy was steadfast in his adherence to piety. He resorted to asceticism to escape life's seduction and delusion. He saw that life really begins when it ends, and that no matter how long a man lives in luxury, he will end up empty-handed but for his good and bad deeds. Ubaiy much contemplated life and once said, "Man's food is a good example of what life is all about, for no matter how much you are careful that it tastes delicious and that its ingredients are well proportioned, look what it turns in to after you digest it."

Whenever Ubaiy addressed people, he was like a magnet that attracted their attention and interest. He feared no one but Allah and desired nothing of life. When Islam gained more lands and influence, he saw that Muslims flattered their rulers. So, he warned them by saying, "They are ruined and will ruin others. I don't pity them, but I pity the Muslims that they will ruin."

His extreme piety and fear of Allah made him cry whenever Allah or the Day of Judgment was mentioned. The noble Quran's verses shook his heart and soul whenever he recited them or he heard them recited. One verse in particular would make him incredibly sad: *He has the power to send torment on you from above or from under your feet, or to cover you with confusion in party strife, and make you to taste the violence of one another.* (6:65)

The thing that Ubaiy most dreaded was that one day the Islamic nation would suffer turmoil and violence at the hands of its own sons. He always asked for Allah's safety and protection. He won it by Allah's mercy, and he met Allah as a true believer who felt completely secure in his reward.

(45)

SA'AD IBN MUAD

Rejoice, Abu Amr!

Sa'ad ibn Muad committed himself to Islam at the age of 31 and achieved martyrdom at 37. Those seven years before his death were extremely difficult for Sa'ad (may Allah be pleased with him), as he exerted all his energy in the service of Allah and His Messenger ﷺ.

Do you see that handsome, gallant, and tall man with a radiant face? He is the one we are here for - Sa'ad. He runs quickly to see a man from Makkah. His name is Musab ibn Umair, sent by Muhammad ﷺ to Medina to call people to commit themselves to Islam and monotheism. Initially, Sa'ad was going there to drive this stranger out of Medina along with his religion. But, no sooner had he approached Musab's assembly at the house of his nephew, Asad ibn Zurarah, than his heart was revived by a pacifying breeze. No sooner had he reached those men who gathered there, taken his place among them and listened intently to Musab's words, than Allah guided him to the right path that illuminated his soul. In one of the incredible miracles of fate, the leader of the Ansar put aside his spear and shook hands with Musab, as a sign of his allegiance to the Prophet ﷺ.

A new sun shone on Medina that day, as soon as Sa'ad ibn Muad committed himself to Islam. It would encompass many hearts in the sphere of Islam later on. Sa'ad committed himself to the new faith and withstood the hardships that ensued with much heroism. When the Prophet ﷺ emigrated to Medina, the houses of Banu Al-Ashhal (Sa'ad's tribe) welcomed the Muhajirun, and their money was utterly at their disposal without arrogance, abuse, or limitation.

When the Battle of Badr was about to take place, the Prophet ﷺ gathered his Companions, both Ansar and Muhajirun, to consult them on the preparations for war. His amiable face turned towards the Ansar and he addressed them saying, "I want to know your opinion about what should be done concerning the imminent battle."

Sa'ad ibn Muad stood up and said "O Prophet of Allah, we firmly believe in you, and we witness that what descends on you is the truth. We swore a solemn oath and pledged you allegiance, so go ahead with whatever you want, and we shall stand by your side. We swear by Allah

Who Has sent you with the truth that if you reach the sea and cross it, we will cross it hand in hand with you. No man will lag or stay behind. We are ready to go to war against our enemy tomorrow, for we are given to terrible warfare, and we are sincere in our desire to meet Allah. I hope that Allah will make us do what will make you proud of us. So, go on with whatever is in your mind. Allah blesses you."

Sa'ad's words made the Prophet's face brighten with satisfaction and happiness as he addressed the Muslims and said, "Rejoice, for Allah promised me one of the two parties of the enemy (either the army or the caravan). By Allah I can almost see with my own eyes where each one of the enemy will be killed."

As we know, at the later Battle of Uhud the Muslims lost control when they dispersed and were taken by surprise by the disbelievers. Amidst the mayhem however, Sa'ad ibn Muad stood firm as if pinned to the ground next to the Prophet ﷺ. There too, Sa'ad defended him courageously as a noble warrior that he was.

The Battle of Khandaq came as a suitable opportunity for Sa'ad to show his admirable valour. This battle came about as a result of the shrewd and deceitful schemes that the Muslims faced from those in their midst. For while the Prophet ﷺ and his Companions were living in Medina in peace, hoping that the Quraysh would refrain from further hostility, a group of Jewish leaders secretly headed for Makkah to instigate the Quraysh against the Prophet. They pledged to help the Quraysh if they decided to raid Medina. They made an agreement with them and even laid down a battle plan. Moreover, on their way home they invited Banu Ghatfan - one of the largest Arab tribes at the time - to join forces with the Quraysh army.

The war plan was ready and everyone knew their role. The Quraysh and Ghatfan were to attack Medina with an enormous army. Meanwhile, the Jews were set to sabotage their own city with a simultaneous attack.

When the Prophet ﷺ discovered their scheme, he resorted to counterplot. First, he ordered his Companions to dig a trench around Medina to hold back the attackers. Second, he sent Sa'ad ibn

Muad and Sa'ad ibn Ubadah to Kab ibn Asad (the leader of Banu Quraidhah), to learn exactly where they stood concerning the imminent war. At that time, mutual agreements and treaties had already been signed between the Prophet ﷺ and the Jews of Banu Quraidhah. The two messengers of the Prophet met with the Jewish leader, and to their surprise he denied the agreements saying, "We did not sign any agreement or treaty with Muhammad."

It was hard for the Prophet ﷺ to expose the people of Medina to such a deadly invasion and exhausting siege; therefore, his only answer was to neutralise Ghatfan, thereby diminishing the size of the attacking army by half its strength. He began to negotiate with the Ghatfan leaders so that they would forsake the Quraysh in exchange for one third of Medina's crops. The leaders of Ghatfan accepted these terms, and both parties agreed to sign an agreement shortly.

The Prophet ﷺ could not go any further without consulting his Companions. He valued Sa'ad ibn Muad and Sa'ad ibn Ubadah's opinion, for they were the leaders of Medina and had the right to a say in any decision that affected it. The Prophet ﷺ told them about his negotiations and that he had resorted to this compensation lest Medina and its inhabitants be exposed to a dangerous attack and siege. Both Sa'ads asked the Prophet, "Is it a matter of choice or is it an inspiration from Allah?" The Prophet ﷺ answered, "It is actually a matter that I chose for you. By Allah, I only do this because I can clearly see that the Arabs joined forces to strike you as one man so I want to curb their strength."

Sa'ad ibn Muad had an intuition that their fate as men and believers was being subtly tested so he said, "O Messenger of Allah, when we and those Jews were disbelievers and polytheists, they did not even dream of eating a date from our land unless we gave it to them out of generosity, hospitality, or for trade purposes. So how is it, after Allah has guided us to Islam and made us honoured by it and by you, that we give them our money? By Allah, we can do without this agreement, and we will give them nothing but warfare until Allah settles our dispute." The Prophet ﷺ at once changed his mind and notified Ghatfan's leaders that his Companions rejected the proposed agreement and that he approved and supported their opinion.

A few days later Medina was subject to a horrible siege. It was, in fact, a siege which the city had brought upon itself due to the trench that was dug as a protection. However, the Muslims were prepared for war. Sa'ad ibn Muad marched around with his weapons, reciting lines of poetry that said, "I waited anxiously for the battle to start. How beautiful death seems when the time is the right."

During one of the battle's encounters, Sa'ad's arm was showered with the arrows, and he bled heavily from his wounds. He received medical care to stop the bleeding, then the Prophet ﷺ ordered him to be carried to the mosque where a tent was put up so that he would be near the Prophet while he was nursed. The Muslims carried their great hero into the Prophet's mosque and Sa'ad looked up to the sky saying, "O Allah our Lord, if the war against the Quraysh is to last any longer, please do let me live a little while longer to fight against them, for I like nothing better than fighting those people who hurt Your Prophet, disbelieved him, and even drove him to emigrate. But if the war has already ended, please make my wounds pave my way to martyrdom. I implore You, dear Allah, not to let me die until I avenge myself upon Banu Quraidhah!"

Allah fulfilled his supplication. His injury caused his death a month later, but he did not die until he had taken his revenge on the Jews of Banu Quraidhah. After some time, the Quraysh became desperate and with their soldiers were gripped by panic from the siege and battle, they took their arms and returned to Makkah disappointed.

The Prophet ﷺ believed that Medina had been compromised by the treachery of the Jews for too long. They left the Muslims in the lurch whenever they chose, a thing that the Prophet could no longer accept. Therefore, he ordered his Companions to march towards Banu Quraidhah, and there the Muslims besieged them for 25 days. When the Jews were certain that there was no escape from the Muslims, they pleaded with the Prophet ﷺ to let Sa'ad ibn Muad, their ally in pagan times, decide what would become of them.

The Prophet ﷺ sent his Companions to bring Sa'ad from his tent at the mosque. He came on a camel and looked very pale and sick. The Prophet addressed him, "Sa'ad, decide what should be done to Banu Quraidhah." Sa'ad remembered their deceit over the years and at the Battle of Khandaq in particular, when Medina had come close to ruin. He said, "I say kill their warriors, capture their children, and distribute their money." Their repeated treachery had come at a difficult price.

Sa'ad's wounds became worse with each passing day. One day, the Prophet ﷺ visited Sa'ad and found him on the verge of death, so he cradled his head in his lap and called upon Allah, "O Allah, Our Lord, Sa'ad has striven hard in the way of Allah. He believed in Your Prophet and did his very best. So please do accept his soul with goodly acceptance." The words of the Prophet ﷺ fell like coolness on the departing soul. Sa'ad strove to open his eyes, hoping that the last face he saw would be the Prophet's and said, "Peace be upon you, Prophet. I do witness that you are indeed the Messenger of Allah."

The Prophet ﷺ took a farewell look of Sa'ad's face and said, "Rejoice, Abu Amr." Abu Sa'id Al-Khudri (may Allah be pleased with him) said, "I was one of those who dug Sa'ad's grave, and each time we dug out a layer of sand, we smelled musk. This went on until we reached his burial niche." Sa'ad's death was a tragic loss for the Muslims. Their only consolation was when they heard the Prophet ﷺ say, "The throne of the Most Beneficent shook when Sa'ad ibn Muad died."

(46)

SA'AD IBN UBADAH

The Carrier of the Ansar's Standard

It is nearly impossible to discuss Sa'ad ibn Muad without mentioning Sa'ad ibn Ubadah too. Both were leaders of Medina. Sa'ad ibn Muad was the leader of the Al-Aws tribe and Sa'ad ibn Ubadah of the Al-Khazraj. Again, both were foremost in their embrace of the Islamic faith. They witnessed the Pledge of Aqabah and lived next to the Prophet ﷺ as obedient soldiers and sincere believers.

Sa'ad ibn Ubadah held a special position amongst the Ansar in that he had also been tortured at the hands of the Quraysh when he had visited Makkah. The Quraysh tortured Makkan Muslims by rote, but to torture a man from Medina was unusual. And, as Ibn Ubadah was a distinguished and influential leader at that, his torture had been out of turn for the Quraysh.

But, how had it happened? After the Pledge of Aqabah was concluded in secret and the Ansar were getting ready to travel home, the Quraysh found out about the Ansar's new agreement with the Prophet ﷺ. Their allegiance now allowed the Prophet to emigrate with his Companions to Medina to flee the power of polytheism and seek sanctuary there. Upon hearing this, the Quraysh lost all self-control. They began hunting all those who pledged allegiance to the Prophet ﷺ.

The disbelievers captured Sa'ad ibn Ubadah, tied his hands to his neck with his saddle girths, and dragged him back to Makkah, where they beat and tortured him. How could this happen to Sa'ad ibn Ubadah though? He was the leader of Medina who always helped any of the Quraysh when in need, protected their trade, and was hospitable to them whenever they visited. Those who captured and abused him may not have known who he was; but even if they had known, it may have made no difference. After all, they readily tortured the elite Muslims of Makkah. Ultimately, the Quraysh had been driven mad by the collapse of their ignorance to the pressure of truth, and they would do all they could to avenge it.

Let us hear the story about his abuse at the hands of the Quraysh, in Sa'ad's own words:

"By Allah, I was in such a terrible state, and at their mercy when I saw a group of people from the Quraysh approaching me. Among them there was this white man who looked as bright as daylight, so I said to myself, 'Well if there is someone among those people left with the least sense of compassion and mercy, then it must be this man'. Unfortunately, as he came

close to me, he raised his fist and punched me severely, so I said to myself that none of them is kind-hearted enough to come to my rescue.

'And there I was - prey in their hands as they dragged me. A man hurried to me and scolded me saying, 'Fie on you! Doesn't anyone of the Quraysh owe you a favour of good neighbourliness?' I answered, 'Yes, of course, I used to help Jubair ibn Mutam's traders and stand by them against those of my people who were unjust to them. I also gave aid to Al-Harith ibn Harb ibn Umaiyah.' Then the man urged me to shout their names and say they owe me the right of good neighbourliness, so I did. Then the man rushed to them and told them, 'A man from Al-Khazraj is being beaten in the valley and he is calling out your names and saying that you owe him the right of good neighbourliness.' They asked him who I was, and as soon as he told them, they told him that everything I said was true and rushed to rescue me."

After this assault, Sa'ad left Makkah. It had made him realise the extent of brutality and savageness the Quraysh were willing to exercise against unarmed people, who simply called for truth and peace. However, this assault merely sharpened his will, and he decided to do his utmost to help the Prophet ﷺ and his Companions.

The Prophet ﷺ emigrated to Medina after the hijra of his Companions. There, Sa'ad put his fortune at the disposal of the Muhajirun. Sa'ad was generous by nature and heredity, being the son of Ubadah ibn Dulaim ibn Haritha, who was famous for his generosity in pagan times. Sa'ad's generosity turned into a sign of his deep-rooted and solid faith.

Narrators commented upon his generosity and said, "The Prophet's houses were always full of food sent by Sa'ad." They also mention that men from the Ansar would often invite one, two, or even three Muhajirun over for meals, whereas Sa'ad ibn Ubadah used to invite over 80 of Muhajirun.

Solely for this, Sa'ad always implored Allah to bestow him with more of His good provision and used to invoke, "O Allah, little provision does not suffice me to be righteous or to act righteously." Therefore, it was justifiable for the Prophet ﷺ to supplicate saying, "O Lord, bring Your blessings and mercy on the family of Sa'ad ibn Ubadah."

Sa'ad directed not only his fortune to the service of Islam, but also his energy and skills. He was a skilled marksman. He showed singular spirit of self-sacrifice during the battles under the Prophet's command ﷺ. Ibn Abbas said about him (may Allah be pleased with them both), "The Prophet ﷺ used only two standards each time he was at war: the Muhajirun's flag with Ali ibn Abu Talib, and the Ansar's flag with Sa'ad ibn Ubadah.

Sa'ad was known to be strict in upholding what was right, or what he believed to be his right. If he was convinced about a certain matter, he would publicly support it with an unwavering and uncompromising firmness. This strictness, or even extremism, was the reason why many of his viewpoints which were called into question.

For instance, on the Day of the Conquest of Makkah, the Prophet ﷺ assigned him to lead an army battalion. Hardly had he reached the outskirts of Makkah, the sacred town, when he shouted, "Today is the day of fierce battle. Today is the day of transgression." Umar ibn Al-Khattab heard his threat and hurried to the Prophet and said, "Messenger of Allah, listen to what Sa'ad just said...He should not be entrusted with the command of the battalion that will attack the Quraysh." The Prophet ﷺ gave his assent and ordered Umar to catch up with him and take his place in the command.

It seems that when Sa'ad saw Makkah in a state of surrender and helplessness, he saw flashbacks of the abuse and torture that the believers and he himself had suffered at the hands of its disbelievers. He recalled all the wars they had waged against the Muslims just because of their belief in monotheism. His stern nature made him rejoice at the Quraysh's calamity and seek revenge.

This sternness was also apparent in his famous attitude on the Day of As-Saqifah. After the Prophet ﷺ died, a group of the Ansar met with Sa'ad. They insisted that the Prophet's Caliph should be one of the Ansar, as the caliphate was an honour in both this world and the next. Naturally, they all craved to win that honour. But the Prophet ﷺ had already chosen his Caliph when he asked Abu Bakr to take his place as imam while he was sick. His Companions saw this and other special qualities enjoyed by Abu Bakr as a sign for his right to the caliphate. For instance, Abu Bakr was with the Prophet as they hid in the cave for three nights from the Quraysh during their hijra to Medina. His position in the Prophet's inner circle was obvious.

Umar ibn Al-Khattab and several of his companions stood by Abu Bakr as their choice for the caliphate and held fast to their opinion. On the other hand, Sa'ad ibn Ubadah and his companions took a different view. This angered many of the Prophet's Companions who held Ibn Ubadah responsible for such a dispute.

However, Sa'ad ibn Ubadah was arguably only being true to himself. He always held tenaciously to his convictions and insisted on being outspoken concerning his position on matters. This characteristic came out clearly at the Battle of Hunain, in front of the Prophet. When the Muslims were victorious in battle, the Prophet ﷺ always distributed the spoils of war among all the Muslims. On that particular day though, he took special care of the elite who had committed themselves to Islam only recently, so as to help them discipline themselves by this privilege. He did not give anything to the long-standing Muslims, as he thought that their Islam sufficed them. He also gave to the warriors who were in need. The war booty had become an important source of revenue on which the Muslims relied. Therefore, the Ansar bitterly wondered what made the Prophet deprive them of the booty.

Hassan ibn Thabit, the poet of the Ansar, recited lines of poetry that said:

Go to the Prophet and say you are the best among all human beings. Why should you invite Sulaim tribe to take a share of war spoils although they are mere Muhajirun, while you deprived the Ansar who gave shelter, support and help to [them]? Allah called them the Ansar because they believed in and supported the religion of guidance in the time of fierce struggle and war. They rushed to strive in the way of Allah and endured difficulties and hardships without getting weary or losing faith.

In those lines, the poet of the Prophet and the Ansar expressed quite eloquently the embarrassment and disappointment the Ansar felt when the Prophet gave his Companions the spoils of war and did not give them anything. The leader of the Ansar, Sa'ad ibn Ubadah, realised the dilemma that they were in, as he had heard people talking about it secretly. This did not appeal to him, so urged by his candour, he went immediately to the Prophet ﷺ and said, "O Messenger of Allah, this group of the Ansar are displeased with what you did with the spoils of war. You have distributed war booty among your people and were most generous to the Arab tribes, but you did not give the Ansar anything."

Thus, the frank Companion aired his concerns and gave the Prophet a candid account of the situation. The Prophet ﷺ asked him, "What is your opinion about it?" Sa'ad answered with his characteristic bluntness, "I have the same viewpoint as my people." Then the Prophet asked him to gather the Ansar.

When the Prophet ﷺ came to where the Ansar gathered, he looked at their disgruntled faces, and his smile brightened with gratitude. Then he said, "O Ansar, I heard that an incident that happened recently made you feel ill at ease. Now, didn't I find you ignorant and guided you to the way of Allah. Didn't I find you poor and Allah enriched you of His bounty? And didn't I find you enemies and Allah joined your hearts together?"

They answered, "Indeed, Allah and His Prophet are far more generous and better."

The Prophet then said, "Don't you have anything to say?"

They answered, "There is nothing to be said but that Allah and His Prophet have the grace and bounty."

The Prophet ﷺ then said, "By Allah, you could have justly said, 'We believed in you at a time when all called you a liar. We supported you at a time when you were frustrated. We gave you our money at a time when you were poor and we even sheltered you at a time when you were homeless.' O Ansar, are you upset for a thing so trivial and worldly that I gave to some people so as to join their hearts to Islam and left you out of it, believing that your Islam sufficed you? Is it not enough for you that the rest of the people will go home with a sheep or a camel, whereas you will return accompanied by the Prophet's love and appreciation? By Allah, if I were not one of the Muhajirun I would rather be one of the Ansar, and if people moved in different ways, I would choose the way taken by the Ansar. Allah, do have mercy on the Ansar, their children, and their children's children."

By the time the Prophet ﷺ concluded his words; their beards were wet with tears, for the words of the great Prophet filled their hearts with tranquillity and enriched their souls. All of them, including Sa'ad, cried out, "It is enough for us to have the Prophet's love as our reward."

In the first days of Umar's caliphate, Sa'ad went to the Commander of the Faithful and said, with his extreme candour, "By Allah, we prefer your companion Abu Bakr over you. By Allah, I cannot stand to live near you." Umar calmly answered, "Anyone who hates his company should seek a better one elsewhere." Sa'ad said, "I will indeed seek better company somewhere else."

Sa'ad's words to Umar were not an expression of hate or spite. A man who was satisfied with the Prophet's love as his reward could not possibly deny loyalty to such a man as Umar, whom the Prophet ﷺ had always cherished and honoured. It was just that Sa'ad ibn Ubadah did not want to wait for an inevitable dispute between him and Umar. Sa'ad was one of the Companions whom the Quran described as "merciful among themselves." And so, he travelled to Syria. Shortly after, he had settled in the Hauran plateau, Sa'ad returned to his Lord, the Most Merciful, and drew an end to his blessed life.

(47)

USAMA IBN ZAID

The Beloved Son of the Beloved

Once, Umar ibn Al-Khattab, Commander of the Faithful, sat down to distribute money from the treasury among the Muslims. When it was his son's turn, Abdullah ibn Umar, it is narrated that "Umar gave him his share. Then it was the turn of Usama ibn Zaid. Umar gave him double of what he gave his son Abdullah". As Umar gave people according to their merit and endeavour, "Abdullah ibn Umar was afraid that his position was not as highly acknowledged as he desired - to be one of the closest to Allah through his obedience, endeavour, piety, and ascetism." Therefore, Abdullah asked his father, "You preferred Usama, although I experienced with the Messenger of Allah what he did not." Umar answered, "Usama was more beloved by the Prophet ﷺ than you were, and his father was more beloved by the Prophet than your father was."

Who was it, together with his father, that was so close to the Prophet's heart and love? It was a high position which Ibn Umar did not reach, nor even did his father, Umar himself. Who was Usama ibn Zaid, who has been called among the Prophet's Companions 'The Beloved Son of the Beloved'?

His father was Zaid ibn Haritha, the Prophet's servant, who preferred the Prophet ﷺ over his own father, mother, and kin. He was with him when the Prophet stood in front of a large group of Companions saying, "I let you bear witness that Zaid is my son, inheriting from me and I inheriting from him." His name remained Zaid ibn Muhammad until the practice of child adoption was abolished by the Quran.

Usama was Zaid's son. His mother was Umm Ayman, the Prophet's servant and nurse maid. Usama's physical appearance was simple and unimpressive. But, was it not the Prophet ﷺ who said, "It may be that a Muslim's hair is unkempt, his feet covered with dust and his clothes are not neat, but, what if he swore by Allah that he would fulfil his oath?"

His appearance has no weight in Islam. Let us instead take stock of his loyalty. How was his devotion, his virtue? How was his honesty, his piety? Most impressive by all accounts, as Usama was worthy of the Prophet's adoration: "Usama ibn Zaid is the most beloved to me and I wish him to be one of the virtuous. I recommend you to treat him well."

Usama (may Allah be pleased with him) had many great characteristics that enabled him to be so close to the Prophet's heart and beloved in his eyes. He was the son of two generous Muslims belonging to the first converts to Islam who, at the same time, were also the closest and most loyal to the Messenger of Allah ﷺ.

As one of the true sons of Islam, he was nurtured from his first days by Islam alone, without being tainted by the pagan period. Despite his tender age, he was a firm believer and a staunch Muslim, who fulfilled all the duties of his faith with inherent loyalty and an unbreakable will. With intellect and humility, his devotion to Allah and His Prophet ﷺ was limitless.

Furthermore, he represented the victims of all kinds of discrimination who were saved by Islam. He had a darker complexion and was simple featured, and of course he attracted the affection of the Prophet ﷺ immensely. Islam had corrected human norms by dealing with discrimination against such people: *Surely the most honourable of you in the sight of Allah is the most pious of you.* (49:13)

Among the most victorious days of Islam was the Conquest of Makkah. On that day, on the Prophet's right and left were Bilal and Usama, two richly dark-skinned brothers of Islam. In a society where racism was rife, Allah's word had elevated their status to its rightful place. Their pure and virtuous hearts had made them deserving of all kinds of merit.

Usama had not yet reached the age of 20, when the Prophet ﷺ ordered him to be head of an army, leading soldiers that included Abu Bakr and Umar. Discontent spread among some who found it too much for a youth such as Usama to command an army that included many Muhajirun and senior Ansar. Their whispers reached the Messenger of Allah ﷺ, so he ascended his pulpit, thanked and praised Allah and then said, "Some people criticised Usama's army command; they criticised his father's command before him. His father deserved to be the commander as well as Usama. He is the most beloved to me next to his father, and I hope he is among the virtuous ones. I request you to treat him well."

The Prophet ﷺ died before the army set off towards its destination, however the Prophet had left his wise testament to his Companions: "Fulfil Usama's commission. Fulfil Usama's commission." Despite the Prophet's death, Abu Bakr Al-Siddiq, the first Caliph, insisted upon fulfilling that testament. Usama's army set off to its destination; the Caliph only requested that Usama allow Umar to stay behind to be with him in Medina.

At the same time, the Roman (Byzantine) emperor heard the news of the Prophet's death and that an army headed by Usama ibn Zaid was attacking the borders of Syria. He could not hide his astonishment and wonder about the strength of the Muslims, whose plans had not been affected by the Prophet's death. Consequently, the Romans abstained from utilising the Syrian borders as a springboard for Islam's centre in the Arabian Peninsula. Their power therefore, soon began to shrink. Usama's army returned safely without any casualties. The Muslims confessed, "We've never seen a safer army than Usama's."

Usama was personally taught a very difficult, but key life lesson by the Prophet ﷺ. Usama always lived according to its wisdom. It took place two years before the Prophet's death, when Usama was sent by the Prophet to lead a detachment. It was the first time that Usama had been appointed to lead such a mission, and he was tasked with stopping a group of polytheists launching an attack on the Muslims. He accomplished his duty successfully and victoriously. News of his victory preceded his arrival, and the Prophet ﷺ was indeed glad.

Let us leave the rest of the story to be narrated by Usama himself: "When I reached the Prophet ﷺ, the proclamation of good news had already reached him. The Prophet's face beamed jubilantly. He asked me to sit closer to him and said, 'Tell me.' I went on telling and narrating. I mentioned to him that at one point the polytheists were defeated and I could reach a man, at whom I pointed my spear. The man said, 'There is no god but Allah. Nevertheless, I pierced and killed him with my lance. The Prophet's attitude changed. He said, 'Woe unto you! How dare you do that when he said, 'There is no god but Allah'. Woe unto you! How dare you do that when he said, 'There is no god but Allah'.' He continued saying that to such an extent that I wished to rid myself of all my deeds and embrace Islam afresh on that day. No, by Allah, I will never fight anyone saying, 'There is no god but Allah', after what I have heard from the Prophet ﷺ."

Usama was guided by the wisdom of this lesson throughout the remainder of his life. This lesson reveals the Prophet's humanity, his justice, his principles, the greatness of his faith and manners.

Despite the fact that it was a polytheist warrior who had been killed by Usama, the killing was much regretted by the Prophet ﷺ. The warrior had pronounced, "There is no god but Allah," whilst still holding a sword fresh with the blood and flesh of the Muslims. He may well have said those words to save himself or give him another chance to resume fighting. Nevertheless, because he said it, his blood had become inviolate. In that moment, whatever his intention may have been, he deserved security. Usama understood the lesson fully. If the Prophet ﷺ forbids the killing of such a man, what of a war with actual believers and true Muslims? It was for this reason that Usama held an entirely neutral position during the civil strife between Imam Ali and Muawiyah.

Usama loved Ali very much and could see the truth on his side. But, after having been blamed by the Prophet ﷺ for the murder of a polytheist who had simply uttered, "There is no god but Allah," how could he ever kill a Muslim who certainly believed in Allah and His Prophets? Therefore, he sent a message to Ali saying, "If you were in a lion's jaw, I would love to enter it with you. But I've never seen a situation like this before."

He kept indoors during the whole war. When some of his companions came to argue with him over his decision, he simply said, "I will never fight anyone saying, 'There is no god but Allah'."

Once, a companion cited the following verse to him: *And continue fighting them until there is no more persecution and God's religion prevails* (2:193). He replied, "Those are the polytheists [it speaks of] and we fought them until there wasn't any persecution and Allah's religion prevailed."

In 54 AH Usama longed to meet with Allah. On that day, the gates of Paradise opened to receive one of the most reverent and pious believers.

(48)

ABDUR RAHMAN IBN ABU BAKR

A Hero to the End

Abdur Rahman ibn Abu Bakr was the true embodiment of Arab chivalry. His father was Abu Bakr Al-Siddiq, the first convert outside of the Prophet's household, an incomparable believer, and one of 'the two who were in the cave' on the Prophet's hijra to Medina. Despite all that, his son, Abdur Rahman, stuck firmly to the pagan religion of his clan and to the idols of the Quraysh.

At the Battle of Badr, he fought on the side of the Quraysh, against his father. During the Battle of Uhud he was in the forefront of the spearmen recruited by the Quraysh to combat the Muslims. Before any fight, there was always a traditional duel with single, man-to-man combat. Abdur Rahman stepped forward to ask the Muslims who they had chosen to fight him. His father, Abu Bakr, rushed out ready to fight his son. However, the Prophet ﷺ held him back. Such was their relationship in the early days of Islam.

Any true Arab is primarily characterised by his loyalty to his convictions. Being convinced by an idea (even if false), can mean being enslaved by that conviction; there is no way to rid one's self of it, unless a new truer conviction fills one's mind.

Abdur Rahman had a great deal of respect for his father, he trusted his father's rationality. Despite all this, his loyalty to his conviction proved to be superior to his own rationale. His father's conversion to Islam did not tempt him to alter his conviction. He remained unchanged, carrying out the responsibilities of his own faith, defending the idols of the Quraysh and fighting under their standard, in the way that brave warriors do.

But, with such noble men, truth does prevail eventually, no matter how long it takes. Their innate goodness, and the light of their sincerity soon guides them. One day, Abdur Rahman opened his eyes to the light of guidance. He could suddenly visualise Allah in all that surrounded him. It was here that guidance deepened its roots within his soul, it was here that he became a Muslim.

Without delay he set off to meet the Prophet ﷺ. Abu Bakr's face beamed with happiness and delight seeing his son swearing the oath of allegiance to the Prophet ﷺ. He had been a true polytheist, but now he was a true Muslim. No greed or fear had pushed him to Islam; just a rational, rightly-guided conviction blessed by Allah's wisdom. Soon, he started to replace previous deeds with his constant striving in the cause of Allah.

During the Prophet's time, and during the era of the Caliphs who succeeded him, Abdur Rahman never missed a battle. His efforts on the Day of Yamama will never be forgotten. His bravery played a great role in achieving victory against Musailamah's army. It was he, Abdur Rahman, who killed Muhkam ibn At-Tufail, Musailamah's main, scheming guard inside the castle of the apostate army. As soon as Muhkam fell at Abdur Ar-Rahman's hands, all those around him scattered, exposing an opening to the Muslim warriors.

Under the standard of Islam, Abdur Rahman's habits only became brighter. He was loyal to his conviction, completely determined to carry out and follow what was right, and he refused all kinds of flattery. All these manners were the essence of his personality. He never abandoned his principles, even when tempted by desire or influenced by fear. Even on that terrible day, when Muawiyah decided to force a pledge to his son, Yazid, by the sword.

On that day, a message was sent to Marwan, the governor of Medina. It included an oath of allegiance to be read aloud in the mosque, so that all the Muslims would hear it. Marwan did what was ordered. When he finished reading it, Abdur Rahman ibn Abu Bakr turned the atmosphere of silence and despondence in the mosque, into one of loud opposition by saying, "By Allah, it's not the welfare of Muhammad's nation that you are seeking. On the contrary, you want to turn it into a Heraclian rule. When Heraclius dies another follows."

Abdur Rahman could clearly see the dangers awaiting Islam if Muawiyah was to carry out his desire. He could see how the transfer of power within Islam was changing from one based on national consultation (by which the nation chooses its leader), to one of autocracy (by which emperors are imposed upon the people, one after another).

Abdur Rahman had hardly finished these words of resistance when a group of Muslims hurried to support him. Leading them were Al-Hussain ibn Ali, Abdullah ibn Az-Zubair and Abdullah ibn Umar. However, at a later point in time, for some compelling reason, they all were forced to hold a position of silence on the subject of Muawiyah's forced pledge of allegiance.

But Abdur Rahman continued to resist loudly. Muawiyah sent him 100,000 dirhams in the hope of pleasing him. Ibn Al-Siddiq threw the money back and said frankly to Muawiyah's messenger, "Go back to him and tell him, it's not Abdur Rahman who is going to buy his life by losing his faith." As soon as he heard the news that Muawiyah had set off towards Medina, Abdur Rahman left for Makkah.

Allah wanted to save him from the temptation of such a situation. Abdur Rahman had hardly reached the borders of Makkah when his soul submitted itself to Allah. Men carried his body to be buried in Makkah. A city which had witnessed his pagan past, but also seen his conversion to Islam; the conversion of an honest, free, and brave man.

sain Ibn Ali, Abdullah Ibn Az-Zubair and Abdullah ibn Umar. However, at a later point in time, for some compelling reason, they all were forced to hold a position of silence on the subject of Mu'awiyah's forced pledge of allegiance.

But Abdur Rahman continued to resist loudly. Mu'awiyah sent him 100,000 dirhams in the hope of placating him. Ibn Al-Siddiq threw the money back and said frankly to Mu'awiyah's messenger, "Go back to him and tell him, it's not Abdur Rahman who is going to buy his life by losing his faith." As soon as he heard the news that Mu'awiyah had set off towards Madina, Abdur Rahman left for Makkah.

Allah wanted to save him from the temptation of such a situation. Abdur Rahman had hardly reached the borders of Makkah when his soul submitted itself to Allah. Men carried his body to be buried in Makkah. A city which had witnessed his pagan past, but also seen his conversion to Islam: the conversion of an honest, free, and brave human.

(49)

ABDULLAH IBN AMR IBN AL-AS

The Submissive Returner to Allah!

The submissive, repentant worshipper we meet here is Abdullah ibn Amr ibn Al-As. Just as his father was famous for his rationality and impressive cunning, his son was equally famous for his high status among worshippers. His whole life was devoted to worship. Days and nights were not enough for his prayer.

He embraced Islam before his father, and since that day, his heart filled with the light of obedience to Allah. Abdullah devoted himself to reciting and understanding the glorious Quran, so that when it was completely revealed he would have learned it all by heart. He did not merely recite it, but rather he lived according to its laws. He then dedicated himself to Quranic recitation and understanding, walking pleasantly through its mellow orchards and taking in the fruit of its verses.

Abdullah was created purely for worship. Nothing could distract him from what he was created for and guided to. If the army of Islam waged jihad against the polytheists who had been attacking them, he could always be found in the front rows, ready to die as a martyr. When the war was over, where was he to be found? There in the great mosque, or even in the small mosque beside his house; fasting in the daytime and praying at night. His tongue did not know any worldly talk, no matter how legitimate. His tongue knew only how to invoke Allah, recite the Quran, praise Him, and ask for His forgiveness.

It is worthwhile to know how deep his worship and asceticism was. The Prophet ﷺ once found himself forced to interfere in order to limit Abdullah's excessive worship. Therefore, the moral which can be taken from Abdullah's life is twofold. On the one hand, it demonstrates how one's soul can reach the utmost degrees of devotion, worship, and virtue. On the other hand, it demonstrates Islam's concern to maintain moderation, even when perfection is aspired to; lest that soul should lose its zeal to maintain a healthy body in the process.

It reached the Prophet ﷺ that Abdullah spent his life in a uniform manner. If there was no battle to join, then he would spend his time in non-stop worship, fasting, prayer, and recitation of the Quran. The Prophet sent for him, appealing to him to be moderate. He ﷺ said, "Is it true what I heard, that you fast every day without eating (without breaking your fasting by one or two days) and that you pray all night without sleeping? It's enough to fast just three days every month." Abdullah said, "I can bear more than that!" The Prophet ﷺ said, "It's enough to fast two days each week." Abdullah said, "I can bear more than that." The Prophet ﷺ said, "Then, why don't you fast the best fasting of all, Dawud's (David's) fast; he fasted one day and ate on the other."

The Prophet ﷺ continued asking him, " I've been informed that you recite the whole Quran in one night. I'm afraid when you get older you will feel bored reciting it. Recite it once each month. Recite it once every ten days. Recite it once every three days." Then he said, "I fast and eat. I pray and sleep. I marry women. Whoever abstains from following my path, indeed, is not of me." Abdullah lived long and when he got older and weaker, he always remembered the Prophet's words and lamented, "If only I had accepted the Prophet's advice."

It is not easy to find a believer of that sort engaged in a war fought by two Muslim parties against each other. So, how is it that he joined Muawiyah's army in the battle against Imam Ali? But, the more we contemplate Abdullah's position, the more we understand his logic and respect his opinion.

We saw how Abdullah was engaged in worship in a way which nearly endangered his life. His father was always concerned about this, and so he often complained to the Prophet ﷺ. On that particular instance when the Prophet asked Abdullah to be moderate in worship, Abdullah's father, Amr, was present. The Prophet ﷺ put Abdullah's hand into his father's saying, "Do as I ordered you and obey your father."

Although Abdullah was obedient to his father because of his faith, the Prophet's order to him in such a way and on such an occasion had a very profound impact on him. Abdullah lived his whole life always remembering this short statement, "Do as I ordered you and obey you father."

Days and years passed. Muawiyah in Syria refused to swear the oath of allegiance to Ali. Ali refused to submit to an illegal rebellion. War broke out between the two Muslim parties. The Battle of Jamal passed, and now it was the turn of As-Siffin. Abdullah's father, Amr ibn Al-As, chose to fight on Muawiyah's side. Knowing how much people trusted and acknowledged his son's faith, Amr found it very beneficial for Muawiyah's party to convince Abdullah to engage in the war on their side. In addition, Amr was always optimistic whenever he had Abdullah beside him in times of war. He could not forget their conquest of Syria and the Day of Yarmuk.

When he intended to set out towards Siffin, Amr appealed to his son saying, "O Abdullah, get ready, you're going to fight with us." Abdullah replied, "How? The Prophet ﷺ has entrusted me never to hold a sword to a Muslim's neck." By means of his cleverness, Amr tried to convince his son that they just intended to kill Uthman's murderers and to take revenge.

Then he surprised his son with the following words, "O Abdullah, do you remember the last thing the Prophet committed you to, when he put your hand over mine saying, 'Obey your father'? I order you now to join us and fight with us."

Abdullah went obediently with his father, but with the deep intention to neither carry a sword, nor kill a Muslim. But how was that going to be possible? For the time being, he was just joining his father; but when the fight started, he hoped to let Allah do as He willed.

It was a hard and fierce battle. Historians argue and differ on whether Abdullah actually joined the fray from the very beginning or not. We are of the opinion that he did join from the start, because the battle had hardly begun when something happened which forced Abdullah to stand clearly against the whole war, and against Muawiyah.

Ammar ibn Yasir, who was well respected by the Companions, was fighting on the side of Imam Ali. Once, in the past the Prophet ﷺ had foreseen Ammar's murder. This was in the days when the Prophet and the Companions were building their mosque at Medina after the hijra. As we have aforementioned in his biography, the rocks being used for the mosque were enormous, and near impossible to carry more than one at a time. However, Ammar was so cheerful and glad that he went on carrying two rocks at a time. The Prophet ﷺ looked at him with tearful eyes saying, "Woe upon the son of Sumaiyah. He is going to be killed by the unjust party." All the Companions who took part in the building heard the prophecy and remembered it well. Abdullah ibn Amr was one of those who heard it.

At the beginning of the battle between Ali and Muawiyah's parties, Ammar ascended a hill shouting, "Today is the day that we are going to meet Muhammad and his Companions." A group of Muawiyah's party committed themselves to killing Ammar, so they pierced him with a lance, whereby he fell as a martyr. The news of Ammar's death spread rapidly. Abdullah stood up agitated, and said, "Is it true that Ammar has been killed ? Did you do it? That means you are the unjust party! You are the misled warriors!" Like a portent he burst into the army, discouraging the fighters, shouting loudly, "You are the unjust party as long as it's you who killed Ammar. The Prophet ﷺ foresaw his murder by the unjust party some 27 years ago."

Abdullah's words soon reached Muawiyah, who sent for Amr and his son. He said to Amr, "Can't you stop your mad man?" Abdullah said, "I'm not mad, but I heard the Prophet ﷺ once saying to Ammar, 'You will be killed by the unjust party'.' Muawiyah continued asking, "Why, then, did you join our party?" Abdullah said, "Because the Prophet ﷺ asked me to obey my father and I obeyed him in joining you, but I didn't fight."

While they were arguing, someone entered asking Muawiyah to permit the entrance of Ammar's murderer. At that moment Abdullah shouted, "Let him in and announce the 'good news' he is in hell." On hearing this, Muawiyah lost his temper. He shouted to Amr, "Can't you hear what he is saying?" Abdullah said that he spoke only the truth and that Ammar's murderers were no more than unjust tyrants. Then he turned to his father and said, "Had it not been for the Prophet's order to obey you, I would not have gone out with you."

While inspecting their army, Muawiyah and Amr were terrified to hear all the people talking about the Prophet's prophecy to Ammar: "You are going to be killed by the unjust party." Amr and Muawiyah were afraid of a revolt, so they devised a cunning trick. They spread the following words among the people: "Yes, the Prophet ﷺ said to Ammar on that day, 'You'll be killed by the unjust party'. The Prophet's prophecy is true. Ammar has been killed. But who killed him? The true murderers are those who asked him to go out to fight."

In the midst of such a confusing situation, any logic is easily accepted. In this way Muawiyah and Amr's plan prevailed. The battle continued. But, Abdullah retreated to his mosque and to his worship.

Abdullah went on to live a life filled with nothing but worship and adoration. Nevertheless, the mere act of going out to the battlefield that day stayed with him. He never remembered this incident without weeping and saying, "What did I have to do with As-Siffin? Why did I bother myself with the killing of Muslims?"

One day, while Abdullah sitting with some companions in the Prophet's mosque, Hussain ibn Ali (may Allah be pleased with him) passed by and they greeted each other. When Hussain went away Abdullah said to those sitting with him, "Would you like to know the human being most beloved to the angels? It's the one who just passed by, Hussain ibn Ali. He has not talked to me since the Day of As-Siffin. I would like him to talk to me more than I desire all the blessings of this world."

He resolved to visit Hussain with Abu Sa'id Al-Khudri. There at Hussain's house the meeting of these two great men took place. Abdullah began to talk. When he mentioned As-Siffin, Hussain asked him sternly, "You, did you join the fight on Muawiyah's side?" Abdullah said, "One day, Amr ibn Al-As complained to the Prophet ﷺ saying, 'Abdullah fasts the whole day and prays all night.' Then the Prophet said to me, 'O Abdullah, pray and sleep, fast and eat. Obey your father.' When it was the day of As-Siffin, my father swore by Allah that I had to go out with him. I went out, but, by Allah, I didn't pierce with a lance, I didn't fight with a sword and I didn't shoot any arrows."

At the age of 72, whilst praying in his mosque and asking for Allah's forgiveness, Abdullah was invited to his eternal voyage. Filled with much longing, he responded. His soul left the world joyfully to join his brethren who had preceded him. The announcer of good news proclaimed from Heaven, "*O soul at peace, return to your Lord, well pleased and well pleasing. Enter you among My servants, and enter into My Paradise!*" (89:27-30)

(50)

ABU SUFYAN IBN AL-HARITH

From Darkness to Light

Here is another Abu Sufyan, a different one than the Abu Sufyan ibn Harb we all know. His story is one of being guided after straying from the path of truth, a story of love after hatred, and of happiness after suffering. It is the story of Allah's infinite mercy and of how it opened the gates to someone seeking Allah's refuge, after a long journey full of hardship.

Can you imagine, Ibn Al-Harith spent 20 years in a continuous fight against Islam! 20 years from the beginning of the revelation until the Day of the Conquest. During this whole period Abu Sufyan was encouraging the Quraysh and their allies, by attacking the Prophet ﷺ through satires. His three brothers, Nawfal, Rabufah, and Abdullah, converted to Islam before him.

The Abu Sufyan whom we are talking about was the cousin of the Prophet ﷺ, as he was the son of Al-Harith ibn Abdul Muttalib. Furthermore, he was the foster brother of the Prophet ﷺ, having been suckled for a few days by Halima Al-Sa'adia, the Prophet's wet-nurse.

One day, destiny called him to meet his happy fate. He called his son Jafar and said to his men that they were both getting ready to travel. "Where to, Ibn Al-Harith? What is your destination?" "To the Messenger of Allah ﷺ to submit ourselves to Allah, Lord of the Worlds."

With a repenting heart he began to ride his horse. At a place called Al-Abuwa, he could see a great army approaching. He soon realised that it was the Prophet ﷺ himself, moving forward to enter Makkah. He began to search for a way out. The Messenger of Allah had already given the Companions permission to shed Abu Sufyan's blood, because of his continuous fight against Islam - a fight in which he had used his sword as well as his tongue.

If anyone in the approaching army saw him, he would no doubt take revenge. Therefore, Abu Sufyan had to find a clever way which would enable him to meet the Messenger of Allah ﷺ first before any other Muslim could see him. He disguised himself, hiding all his features, then took his son and walked a while until he could clearly see the Prophet ﷺ, who at that moment was with a large number of the Companions.

Suddenly, Abu Sufyan threw himself between the Prophet's hands, removing his disguise. As soon as the Prophet ﷺ recognised him, he turned his face. Abu Sufyan turned and approached him from another direction, in vain; the Prophet turned his face again. Abu Sufyan and his son Jafar both shouted, "We bear witness that there is no god but Allah. We bear witness that Muhammad is the Messenger of Allah." They came nearer saying, "O Prophet, no reproach!" The Prophet ﷺ replied, "No reproach shall be upon you, Abu Sufyan." Then the Prophet ﷺ handed him over to Ali ibn Abu Talib and said to him, "Teach your cousin ablution, the Sunnah and take him away right now." Ali took him and soon returned. The Prophet ﷺ told Ali, "Tell people that the Prophet ﷺ is pleased with Abu Sufyan, so be pleased with him."

In that brief moment, Allah ended a period of hardship and error for Abu Sufyan, opening the gates to His infinite mercy. He nearly converted to Islam when, during the Battle of Badr, he saw something that confused him. During that battle Abu Lahab stayed behind, sending Al-As ibn Hisham in his place. Abu Lahab was waiting eagerly to hear news of the battle, when the shocking defeat was announced. He was sitting near the well of Zamzam in the middle of a group of the Quraysh, when a horseman approached. It was Abu Sufyan ibn Al-Harith. Abu Lahab did not give him a chance to rest, but asked him immediately, "Come nearer, my cousin. You have the latest news! How was it?" Abu Sufyan ibn Al-Harith said, "By Allah, we had hardly begun fighting when it was as if we offered them our bodies, let them do with us whatever they wanted, let them fight us as they pleased, took us prisoners as they liked. I swear, by Allah, I do not blame the Quraysh, as we met white men riding piebald horses filling the space between heaven and earth. Nothing is like them, nothing could stop them."

Abu Sufyan surely meant that angels were fighting on the Prophet's side. Why is it then that Abu Sufyan did not submit himself to Allah at that time after having seen what he first described? But, doubt paves the way to certainty. The more obstinate and opinionated his doubt, the firmer and more persistent his conviction. Finally, when the day of his guidance arrived, his conversion brought that certainty to fruition.

From the very beginning, just moments after his conversion, he began to strive to worship as if he was racing against time. He hoped to erase all traces of his past to compensate for all that he had missed. He took part in all the battles after the Day of the Conquest. On the Day of

Hunain for instance, a dangerous trap was prepared by the polytheists. They attacked the Muslims so fiercely that a great deal of Muslim warriors lost their reason and retreated, but the Prophet ﷺ stood firm appealing, "O people, I'm the Prophet...I'm the son of Abdul Muttalib."

During those fearful moments, a small group, not losing their reason, continued fighting. Among them was Abu Sufyan and his son Jafar. Abu Sufyan was holding the bridle of the Prophet's horse, but when he saw what happened, he readied himself for martyrdom and vowed to stay holding the Prophet's horse to keep him safe.

He held the horse's bridle with one hand while cutting the throats of the polytheists with the other. The Muslims regrouped around the Prophet ﷺ and Allah blessed them with victory. Although the fight was over, when the Prophet looked around he could see a faithful believer still holding his horse's bridle. It was Abu Sufyan, who had not left his place since the battle began. The Prophet ﷺ glanced and asked, "Who is it? My brother Abu Sufyan ibn Al-Harith?" Immediately after hearing the word "brother" Abu Sufyan's heart was filled with joy and he rejoiced at their victory together.

After the Prophet's death, Abu Sufyan longed meet his Prophet and return to his Maker. He desired his end so much, that people saw him digging out his own grave at Al-Baqi cemetery. When people expressed their astonishment, he just admitted, "I'm preparing my grave."

Only three days later, Abu Sufyan was lying at home in his death throes with his relatives weeping beside him. When he opened his eyes, he said in complete tranquillity, "Don't cry. I didn't commit a single sin since I converted to Islam." As his head fell upon his chest, he bid his last farewell to the world.

(51)

UMRAN IBN HUSSAIN

A Resemblance to the Angels

It was in the year of Khaibar that Umran turned to the Prophet ﷺ, to swear the oath of allegiance. Since the moment he put his right hand into the Prophet's, his own hand earned respect. He promised himself to use his hands only in the pursuit of virtuous deeds.

Umran was a clear image of honesty, humility, and devotion to Allah. Although he was blessed with a great deal of success, he would often say, "I wish I were ashes dispersed by the wind." God-fearing men of this type did not fear Allah because of their sins. Sins were rarely committed by them after their conversion to Islam. But, the more they got acquainted with Allah's majesty, the more they recognised their inability to truly thank and worship Allah, hence his remarks.

Once the Prophet's Companions asked him, "O Prophet of Allah, why when we are sitting with you do we feel calmness in our hearts… seeing the Hereafter as if it were before us, but when we leave you to meet our wives, children, and our worldly affairs, we deny ourselves?" The Prophet ﷺ responded, "By Allah, if you adhered strictly to your first state, the angels would have shaken your hands clearly. So, it is natural for there to be a worshipping time followed by business."

When Umran heard this Prophetic saying, he promised instead to always strive for this almost unattainable goal, even if it took him his whole life. He was never convinced to live dividing his time one hour for leisure, and one hour for worship. He wanted instead for his life to be a long chain of prayer and total devotion towards the Lord of the Worlds.

During the caliphate of Umar ibn Al-Khattab, he was sent to Basra, to teach its inhabitants the principles of jurisprudence. He settled there, and soon people turned to him to seek his guidance. Al-Hasan Al-Basri and Ibn Sirin said, "No one of the Prophet's Companions who entered Basra can be considered better than Umran ibn Hussain." Umran refused to occupy himself with anything but worship. He spent his whole time doing nothing but devoting himself to Allah, in an almost other worldly sense.

When the great uprising between the parties of Ali and Muawiyah took place, he did not just hold a neutral position, but appealed to people to abstain from joining the fight altogether, adhering to the cause of peace. He went on saying, "I would prefer to be a shepherd on top of a mountain till I die rather than shoot an arrow at anyone in either party, right or wrong." Any Muslim he met, he advised saying, "Keep to your mosque. If it is broken into forcefully, then keep indoors. If the doors are broken into forcefully by someone who aims at taking your life and wealth, then fight him."

Umran ibn Husain's faith reached a very high level. For 30 years he suffered from a severe disease. However, he never complained or showed any signs of discontent. Instead, he adored and worshipped Allah persistently, throughout his life. When his visitors came to encourage him, he always replied, "The dearest things to my heart are those dearest to Allah."

When he felt that death fast approaching, he said to his family and kin, "When you finish burying me, slaughter [an animal] and feed the people." Truly, this was excellent advice. The death of someone like Umran should have been akin to a celebration of sorts, wherein his soul was wedded to Paradise, and to a heaven prepared only for the pious.

(52)

SALAMAH IBN AL-AKWA

The Infantry Hero

His son, Iyas, summarised all Salamah's virtues in just one sentence: "My father never lied." To be described by this singular virtue inevitably elevates a person's status amongst the pious. And, Salamah ibn Al-Akwa thoroughly deserved this high status. He was one of the finest Arab spearmen around and was also famous for his courage and charitable deeds. So, let us learn more about this generous Companion.

Salamah sincerely submitted himself to Islam at the Pledge of Radwan. This took place in 6 AH, when the Prophet ﷺ tried to visit the Sacred House in Makkah with his Companions, but the Quraysh stopped them from doing so. The Prophet sent Uthman ibn Affan ahead to tell the Quraysh that he had come only as a visitor, not a fighter. While they awaited Uthman's return though, a rumour spread that the Quraysh had killed him. The Prophet ﷺ therefore sat under the shade of a tree and took the Companions' oath of allegiance, one by one. They gave him their word that they would be ready to die in the cause of Allah should a battle ensue.

Salamah reported: "I swore the oath of allegiance in front of the Prophet to be ready to die. Then I stepped aside. When the crowd of people nearly ended, the Prophet ﷺ said, 'O Salamah, aren't you going to swear your oath of allegiance?' I said, 'I've already done that.' He said, 'Again.' I swore the oath again."

Salamah had redeemed his oath long before that day. He had redeemed it since the day he professed that there is no god but Allah, and Muhammad is His Messenger. He said, "I joined the Prophet ﷺ in seven battles and joined Zaid ibn Haritha in nine battles." Radwan made a special pledge with the Companions to protect one another and the Prophet, should the occasion arise.

He was one of the most skilful warriors as an infantryman, and one of the best aims with both arrows and spears. His tactics were similar to present day guerrilla warfare: if an enemy approached, he retreated waiting for him to likewise move back or to take a rest, and then he would attack him by surprise. In this way he was able to chase alone the force led by Uyainah ibn Hisn Al-Fizari which raided the environs of Medina in the

Dhi Qarad Raid. Totally alone, he followed their tracks, then continued fighting and pushing them away from Medina until the Prophet ﷺ reached him with reinforcements. On that day the Prophet said to the Companions gathered, "Our best infantryman is Salamah ibn Al- Akwa".

Salamah never knew deep sorrow, except when his brother Amir ibn Al-Akwa died during the Battle of Khaibar. Amir was the one singing in front of the Muslim army:

Had it not been for You
We would not have been guided,
Nor prayed, nor given charity.
Bless us with tranquillity,
And let us be strong and firm-hearted
when meeting our enemies.

In that battle, Amir went to strike a polytheist with his sword, but his sword bent and its edge injured Amir fatally. Some Muslims said, "Poor Amir, he has been deprived of martyrdom." Salamah's anxiety was severe because he thought, like others, that his brother, who had killed himself accidently, was deprived of the recompense of jihad and the reward of martyrdom. But the Prophet ﷺ soon corrected them, when Salamah came to him saying, "O Messenger of Allah, is it true that by dying in this way Amir has been deprived of the reward of all his previous deeds?" The Messenger ﷺ answered, "He has been killed as a mujahid. He is to be granted two rewards. He is right now swimming in the rivers of Paradise."

Salamah was very generous. However, he was more so when asked to give something for the sake of Allah. If someone had asked him to give away his life for the sake of Allah, he would not have hesitated to do so. People knew this attitude of his, so when anyone needed something, he only needed to ask him for it for the sake of Allah. He always said, "If someone would not give for the sake of Allah, for whose sake then would he give?"

On the day of Uthman's murder, the great mujahid realised that the gates of sedition had been opened. How could it be possible for him, who had fought among his brethren all his life, to turn into a warrior against them? It was not his right to use his fighting skills (which had been praised by the Prophet personally) against other Muslim believers. He therefore took his belongings and left Medina for a place called Ar-Rabzah, the same place to which Abu Dhar chose to emigrate and settle.

Salamah spent the rest of his life at Ar-Rabzah. In 74 AH, his burning desire took him to Medina, where he spent one or two days as a visitor, and on the third day he died. It was as if the beloved earth of Medina offered his body a cool, safe shelter to rest in, just as it had offered all his fellow Companions and the virtuous martyrs before him.

(53)

ABDULLAH IBN AZ-ZUBAIR

What a Man, What a Martyr

A blessed child in his mother's womb was he, when Abdullah's mother passed over the burning desert sand, leaving Makkah for Medina on her emigration. While still unborn, Abdullah was destined to emigrate with the Muhajirun. His mother, Asma (may Allah be pleased with her), had hardly reached Quba when she began to suffer labour pains.

Abdullah, the first child to be born after the hijra, was carried to the Prophet's house in Medina. There the Prophet ﷺ kissed him, then chewed a date and rubbed the goodness of it on the newborn's gums (a Sunnah called 'tahnik'). Muslims gathered round, and carried the newborn baby through the streets of Medina applauding and shouting "Allahu Akbar"(Allah is the Greatest).

When the Muslims settled in Medina, some of the Jews there, who bore ill will towards the Muslims, were subdued during the celebrations. They had spread a rumour before that their religious clerics had made the Muslims infertile by means of witchcraft, and that Medina would never witness the birth of Muslim babes. However, when Abdullah was born, he was irrefutable proof from Allah that their claims were mere lies.

Abdullah did not reach the age of maturity during the Prophet's lifetime. However, his close contact with the Prophet ﷺ during his childhood granted him the basic values of manhood. He learnt the principles of life from Muhammad ﷺ himself, principles which would be the subject of people's admiration for many years to come.

As a young boy, Abdullah displayed an extraordinary energy, intellect, and firmness. His youth was full of chastity, worship, and even heroism. As the days went by, his manners did not wane. He was a young man sure of his path, walking his own way with strong will and firm belief in Islam.

By the age of 27, he had already become a war hero during the conquests of Africa, Spain, and Constantinople. His fortitude was especially memorable during the Battle of Ifriqiyah (Tunisia) when 20,000 Muslim soldiers confronted an army of 120,000.

In the midst of the dangerous battle, Abdullah took a look at the enemy's army and soon realised the source of their strength. It was their leader, the Berber king, who galvanised his soldiers, pushing them towards death. Abdullah knew that the battle's outcome depended primarily on the death of their stubborn leader. But how was he going to reach him? He had first to pass through a fierce army.

Abdullah's courage took charge. He called on his companions and said, "Protect my back, attack with me." As sure as an arrow, he forced his way towards the leader, bursting through a wall of ruthless warriors. When he finally reached the king, he struck him down dead. The Muslims soon saw their standard lifted on the same spot where the Berber leader had commanded his soldiers. They realised that victory was near. They strengthened their efforts and soon everything was over in favour of the Muslims. The leader of the Muslim army, Abdullah ibn Abu Sarh was told about the great role Abdullah ibn Az-Zubair had played in their victory. He rewarded him with the honour of personally carrying the news of victory to Medina to the Caliph Uthman ibn Affan.

Nevertheless, his extraordinary heroism came second to his worship. Despite his family, his wealth, his status in society, nothing could hinder Abdullah from his worship - fasting all day long and praying all night.

Umar ibn Abdul Aziz once asked Ibn Abu Mulaikah to describe Abdullah, so he said, "By Allah, I've never seen a soul similar to his. When he began his prayer, he left everything behind. He bowed down and prostrated for such a long period that birds stood on his back considering him a wall, or a gown thrown away. Once a projectile passed between his beard and chest while praying. By Allah, he did not feel it, nor was he shaken by it. He did not stop his recitation, nor hurry his bowing."

Abdullah's sincere worship became noteworthy and features in all accounts of his life. His fasting, his prayer, his pilgrimage, and even his military skills were interwoven threads in his character.

Although there was some kind of disagreement between Abdullah ibn Az-Zubair and Ibn Abbas, the latter still described Abdullah in the following words: "He was a reciter of the Quran, a follower of the Sunnah, submissive to Allah, a God-fearing faster, son of the Prophet's disciple. His mother was Al-Siddiq's daughter, his aunt Aisha (the Prophets wife); his rank can only be ignored by the blind."

Nothing could equal Abdullah's firmness and assiduity. Sincere, noble, strong, he was always ready to sacrifice his life for the sake of his straightforward principles. During his dispute with Banu Umayyah (the Ummayyads) over their attempt to inherit the caliphate, Hussain ibn Numair (the leader of Yazid's army sent to suppress Abdullah's revolt) went to visit Abdullah in Makkah after the news reached there that Yazid had died. Hussain asked Abdullah to go with him to Syria, where he would use his power to force people to swear the oath of allegiance to him after Yazid. However, Abdullah refused this golden opportunity as a matter of principle. Instead, he decided to take repay the Syrian army for the terrible crimes they committed while marching on the Prophet's city of Medina, merely to satisfy the Ummayyads' greed.

We may differ with Abdullah's approach here, wishing he would have preferred peace and forgiveness by accepting Hussain's offer. Regardless, the man's position in favour of his conviction and faith, rejecting lies and tricks, deserves respect.

His resistance against Muawiyah and Yazid was an extraordinary story of bravery. He considered Yazid ibn Muawiyah ibn Abu Sufyan the most unqualified person to rule the Muslim community. That was undeniably true, as Yazid was entirely corrupt. So, how could Abdullah ibn Az-Zubair ever swear the oath of allegiance to him? He strongly refused to do so while Muawiyah was alive, and even more so when his son Yazid became caliph. Yazid sent someone to threaten him. However, Abdullah said, "I'm not going to swear the oath of allegiance to a drunkard."

As the struggle for the caliphate continued to rage, Al-Hajjaj ibn Yusuf soon attacked Makkah on behalf of Abdul Malik ibn Marwan, besieging Abdullah and his men. At that time, among Abdullah's warriors stood a group of very skilful Abyssinian spearmen. Abdullah heard them talking once about the late Caliph Uthman. Their comments about Uthman lacked all fairness. Abdullah reprimanded them severely saying, "By Allah, I don't like to defeat my enemy with the help of someone hating Uthman." So, even at such a crucial time in the midst of Al-Hajjaj's attack, Abdullah sent them away. His sincerity made him indifferent to the loss of 200 of his most skilful spearmen, the faith of whom he could no longer trust. All that, despite the decisive battle which stood before him. The outcome of that battle could perhaps have been very different if those spearmen had remained.

Ibn Az-Zubair eventually became Commander of the Faithful with Holy Makkah as his capital. His rule extended over Hejaz, Yemen, Basra, Kufa, Khurasan, and Syria (except Damascus). The inhabitants of all these provinces swore the oath of allegiance to him. But the Ummayyads were not satisfied. Restless, they waged continuous wars, most of which ended in their defeat. Nothing changed until Abdul Malik ibn Marwan ordered one of the most harsh, criminal and merciless human beings to attack Abdullah in Makkah. This was Al-Hajjaj Ath-Thaqafi, who was described by Umar ibn Abdul Aziz as follows: "If all nations were to weigh together their sins, and we came with only Al-Hajjaj, the balance would sway to our part."

Al-Hajjaj personally led his army to invade Makkah, Ibn Az-Zubair's capital. He besieged it for nearly six months, all the while preventing the provision of water and food in the hope that people would abandon Abdullah. Under the severe pressure of hunger, a large number of fighters surrendered and Abdullah found himself almost alone. Although chances to save his life were still available, he decided to carry out his responsibilities as leader to the very end. He went on fighting with legendary courage, even though he was 70 years old at that time.

We will only grasp the full image of that situation if we listen to the conversation which took place between Abdullah and his mother, the great and noble Asma bint Abu Bakr, a short while before his death. He went to her presenting the whole situation and what seemed to be his destiny. Asma told him, "My son, you know yourself better than anyone else. If you know that you are adhering to the truth and calling to it, then be patient till you die for its sake and don't let the boys of Banu Ummayyah reach your neck. But, if life in this world has been your main concern, then you're a wretched son, destroying yourself and those killed on your side."

Abdullah said, "By Allah, mother, I've never sought life in this world, nor did I submit myself to it. I've never ruled with injustice, treated anyone unfairly, or betrayed anyone." His mother Asma said, "I hope I will receive good consolation if you precede me to Paradise or I precede you. May Allah have mercy for your long prayers at night, your fasting during hot days and your reverent treatment of me and your father. Allah, I've handed over my son to Your fate; I will be pleased with Your destiny. Reward me for sacrificing my son as You reward thankful and patient believers."

They embraced each other and exchanged a farewell look. After one hour of fierce, unparalleled battle, Abdullah received a deadly stroke. Al-Hajjaj, cruel as he was, insisted on beheading and crucifying his lifeless body.

Abdullah's mother, who was 97 years old, went to see her crucified son. Like a towering mountain, his mother stood rooted in front of her son, Abdullah. Just then, Al-Hajjaj himself approached Asma tentatively and said, "O Mother, the Commander of the Faithful, Abdul Malik ibn Marwan, has recommended me to treat you well. Do you need anything?"

She shouted, "I'm not your mother. I'm the mother of that one, crucified on the cross. I don't need you. But I'm going to tell you a hadith which I heard from the Prophet ﷺ. He said, 'He will emerge from Thaqif, a liar and a vicious one.' We have already seen the liar and the vicious one. I don't think he is anyone else, but you."

Having suckled the milk of such an extraordinary mother, it is clear to see that Abdullah could only ever have lived the life he led. A life that reached enormous levels of success, virtue, and heroism.

May peace be upon Abdullah.
May peace be upon Asma.
May peace be upon all the eternally living martyrs.

(54)

ABDULLAH IBN ABBAS

The Nation's Scholar

Ibn Abbas was similar to Ibn Az-Zubair in that both of them were children during the Prophet's era. The Prophet ﷺ died before Ibn Abbas reached manhood. Much like Ibn Az-Zubair, he too bore all the characteristics of maturity in his youth. His principles were guided by the Prophet, who liked him most, praised him often, and taught him nothing but wisdom.

Due to his firm belief, gentle manner, and the richness of his knowledge, he was able to occupy a very high rank among the men around the Prophet ﷺ.

Abdullah ibn Abbas was the son of Al-Abbas ibn Abdul Muttalib ibn Hashim, the Prophet's uncle. His epithet was 'The Nation's Scholar', much deserved due to his versatile knowledge and enlightened mind.

Ibn Abbas came to knowledge at a very early age, a knowledge which only increased as the days went by. That is because the Prophet ﷺ was always nurturing Abdullah. He would often pat Abdullah's shoulders and ask Allah, "O Allah, bless him with the full knowledge of the religion and interpretation of the Holy Quran." The Prophet repeated this same prayer for his cousin in various situations. In this way, Abdullah ibn Abbas realised that he had been moulded to acquire knowledge, and his intellectual capabilities therefore were always that way inclined.

Although he was not older than 13 when the Prophet ﷺ died, he had not spent his childhood in vain. He had attended all the Prophet's assemblies and learned his words by heart. So, when the Prophet passed, Abdullah was eager to learn from the Companions what he had failed to hear or learn from the Prophet ﷺ otherwise. He continually sought knowledge. Whenever he heard that someone had acquired wisdom or learned a hadith by heart, he hurried to learn it from him. His bright and ambitious mind forced him to examine all that passed his ears. He was not just concerned with gathering information, but with examining it and its sources. He once said about himself, "If I wanted to know something about an issue, I would ask 30 Companions."

Abdullah once spoke of own concern to acquire knowledge: "When the Prophet ﷺ died, I said to one of the Ansar youth, 'Let's go to the Prophet's Companions to ask them, as they are still numerous'. He said, 'O Ibn Abbas, how strange you really are! Do you think that people are in need of you while the great Companions are still among them?' The young man dropped the matter, whereas I turned to ask the Prophet's Companions. Whenever I was informed that someone had related a hadith, I would go to [that Companion] in the afternoon while he was napping. I put my gown as a pillow under my head in front of his door. The wind scattered the dust over me. When [the Companion] finished his nap and came out and saw me, he said, 'O Prophet's cousin, what is it that brought you here? Why didn't you send for me?' Then I would say, 'No, it's you who deserves to be visited.' Then I would ask him about the hadith and learn from him."

In this way, young Abdullah went on asking questions repeatedly, then examined the answers and discussed them with an ever-curious mind. Every day his wisdom only grew, until he achieved (while still a youth) the wisdom, patience, and eloquence normally reserved for the elderly. His knowledge was so expansive that the Commander of the Faithful, Umar, was eager to consult with him on every great issue. He called him, "the young leader of the elderly". Ibn Abbas was once asked, "How did you acquire all that knowledge?" He answered, "By means of a questioning tongue and a reasoning mind." It was through this habit that Ibn Abbas became 'The Nation's Scholar'.

Sa'ad ibn Abu Waqqas described him in the following words: "I've never seen one with such presence of mind, nor one more intellectual or milder than Ibn Abbas. I've seen Umar (may Allah be pleased with him), although surrounded by those who attended Badr, inviting him to discuss difficult problems. Whenever Ibn Abbas spoke his view, Umar always stuck to it."

Ubaid Allah ibn Utbah once said of him: "I've never seen anyone more knowledgeable in the Prophet's hadith than Ibn Abbas. Neither did I see anyone more knowledgeable during Abu Bakr, Umar or Uthman's caliphates than him; or more accurate in what he says in terms of jurisprudence, or more knowledgeable in terms of poems, the Arabic language, Quranic interpretation or religious matters. He divided his time, each day teaching one subject or another, jurisprudence, Quranic interpretation, invasions, poems, and history, each one a different day. I've never seen a scholar listening to him without submitting himself completely to him, nor asking without being impressed by his vast and rich knowledge."

Ibn Abbas, who was appointed governor of Basra during the caliphate of Ali ibn Abu Talib (may Allah be pleased with him) was once described by a Muslim brother in the following words: "He stuck to three matters, and gave up three. He dazzled men's hearts whenever he talked. He was a good listener whenever he was spoken to. He chose the easiest of two matters whenever he was opposed. He gave up hypocrisy. He gave up the companionship of wicked people. He gave up all that is excusable."

His cultured, diverse and comprehensive knowledge was admirable. He was the shrewd authority in every field of knowledge: Quranic interpretation, jurisprudence, history, Arabic language and literature. Therefore, those who sought truth, sought him. People travelled to Ibn Abbas in groups from all over the Islamic world, purely to listen to and learn from him.

A Companion who was a contemporary with Ibn Abbas once narrated:

"I've seen one of Ibn Abbas' scholastic assemblies. If the whole tribe of the Quraysh would have been proud, it would have been enough for their pride. I've seen people gathering in front of his door until the whole path had become so crowded that no one could enter or exit.

'I entered, informing him that a great number of people were sitting in front of his door. He asked me to prepare his water for ablution, which he performed, then sat down and said, 'Go out to them and invite those interested in Quranic interpretation.' I went out and let them in. They entered, filling the house. They didn't ask about anything without being answered in a satisfactory manner. Then he said to them, 'Don't forget your brethren'. They went out to allow others to enter. Then he said, 'Go out and invite those interested in jurisprudence'.

I went out and let them enter, filling the house. They didn't ask about anything without being satisfactorily answered. Then he said, 'Don't forget your brethren'. They went out to allow others to enter. Then he said, 'Go out and invite those interested in religious duties'.

'I went out and let them in. They entered, filling the house. They didn't ask about anything without being satisfactorily answered. Then he said, 'Don't forget your brethren'. They went out to allow others to enter. Then he said, 'Go out and invite those interested in the Arabic language and litera-

ture'. I went out and let them in. They entered, filling the house. They didn't ask about anything without being satisfactorily answered."

Ibn Abbas not only had a sharp memory, but an extraordinary one, coupled with fierce intelligence. His arguments were as clear as day. He would not let his opponent leave until he was not only convinced, but completely satisfied with his logic. He did not consider his knowledge a source of pride, but only a vehicle for the truth.

For a long time, his sharp logic had been a source of alarm to the Khawarij. Once, Imam Ali sent him to a large group of the Khawarij. They had a wonderful discussion, where Ibn Abbas dominated the dialogue, and argued in a very admirable way. The following is an extract of that long conversation:

Ibn Abbas asked them, "What do you have against Ali?"

They said, "We are discontent with three matters. First, he let men judge in Allah's religion, whereas Allah said, *...surely judging is only for God.* (6:57) Second, he is a murderer. However, he didn't take any captives or war booty. If they had been disbelievers, then their wealth would have been permissible, and if they had been Muslims, then their murder would have been prohibited. Third, during the arbitration, he agreed to give up the title 'Commander of the Faithful' in response to his enemies. If he isn't Commander of the Faithful, then he must be Commander of the Disbelievers."

Ibn Abbas began to refute their claims. "As for letting men judge in Allah's religion, what's wrong with that? Allah said, *O you who believe! Do not kill animals of the hunt while you are on the Pilgrimage, and whoever of you kills it intentionally, he shall make recompense the equal of what he has killed from the cattle, which shall be judged by two just men among you.* (5:95) Tell me, by Allah, is letting men judge in sparing the Muslim blood not worthier than letting them judge in the case of compensating a killed rabbit that is worth a quarter of a dirham?"

Their leaders hesitated in their speech under the pressure of that sarcastic but decisive logic. Then he continued, "As for your claim that he is a murderer who didn't take prisoners or war booty, did you expect him to take Aisha, the Prophet's wife and Mother of the Faithful, a prisoner and her belongings as booty?" At that moment their faces went blank out of shame and some even tried to cover them with their hands.

Ibn Abbas went on to the third claim. "As for your claim that he agreed to give up the title 'Commander of the Faithful' to give arbitration a chance, let me tell you what the Prophet ﷺ did on the Day of Hudaibiyah. While he was dictating the agreement between him and the Quraysh, he said to the scribe, 'Write: This is what the Messenger of Allah agreed upon.' The representative of the Quraysh said, 'By Allah, if we believed that you were the Messenger of Allah, we wouldn't have hindered you from entering the Sacred House or fought against you.' The Prophet ﷺ then said, 'Then write: This is what Muhammad ibn Abdullah has agreed upon. By Allah, I'm the Messenger of Allah even if you deny that. Write whatever you like'."

The discussion between Ibn Abbas and the Khawarij went on. The discussion had hardly ended when some 20,000 of the Khawarij announced their conviction in what was said and announced the end of their opposition to Ali's imamate.

Ibn Abbas not only possessed a great fortune of knowledge, but also an even greater fortune of manners. He was a great figure in his generosity. He spent his wealth abundantly for the people's sake, with the same willingness with which he shared his knowledge. His contemporaries said, "We've never seen a house more filled with food, drinks, fruits, and knowledge than Ibn Abbas' house."

He possessed a pure soul that never harboured any spite. He never tired of wishing good for others, whether he knew them or not. He said about himself, "Whenever I recited a verse, I wished that all people had acquired the knowledge I've acquired. Whenever I heard about a just ruler ruling fairly, I was filled with delight and prayed for him, although I did not need him. Whenever I heard about rain falling on Muslim land, I was filled with delight although I did not own any livestock grazing on that land."

He was a devoted worshipper, who prayed at night and fasted frequently. You would often see tears streaks on his cheek, because he cried so much whenever he prayed or recited the Quran. Whenever he read a reprimanding verse, or saw the mention of death and resurrection, his tearful laments grew louder still.

In addition, he was honest, brave, and eloquent. He had his own opinions about the dispute between Imam Ali and Muawiyah, which proved his capacity for stratagem. He preferred peace to war, kindness to violence, and logic to compulsion.

When Hussain (may Allah be pleased with him) intended to go to Iraq to fight Ziyad and Yazid, Ibn Abbas did everything he could to stop him. Afterwards, he was informed about his martyrdom. He felt deep grief and kept indoors.

Whenever a dispute between two Muslims arose, he could always be seen carrying the banner of peace and forgiveness. It is true that he himself was eventually involved in the battle between Ali and Muawiyah, where he fought on Ali's side. But he did that because, at the beginning, the war represented a necessary eradication of a movement which was causing a terrible split within the Islamic community. It threatened the unity of the faith and of the believers, leaving him no other choice.

As long as Ibn Abbas lived, he filled the Islamic world with knowledge and wisdom. When he reached the age of 71, he was invited to meet Allah. On the day of his burial, the city of Taif witnessed what would become of a believer who had been promised Paradise. While his body settled safely in its grave, the horizon was shaken by the echo of the truthful divine promise: *O soul at peace. Return to your Lord, well pleased and well pleasing. Enter you among My servants. And enter into My Paradise*! (89:27-30).

(55)

ABBAD IBN BISHR

With Him Was the Light of Allah!

Before hijra, Musab ibn Umair went to Medina. He had been appointed by the Messenger of Allah ﷺ to teach the Ansar, who had already sworn their allegiance to the Prophet, and to lead them in prayer. Abbad ibn Bishr was also present, and was amongst those whose hearts Allah guided towards goodness. So, Musab approached the assembly, and Abbad listened to him, stretching out his right hand to give his oath of allegiance to Islam. From that day on, he took his place among the Ansar, with whom Allah is pleased and they with Him.

The Prophet ﷺ emigrated to Medina after the believers of Makkah preceded him there. Then began the military campaigns in which the forces of good and light clashed with the forces of injustice. In each of these battles, Abbad ibn Bishr was in the front ranks fighting heroically, completely dedicated in heart and soul to the cause of Allah. Perhaps the event which we now narrate will disclose something of the heroism of this great believer.

After the Messenger of Allah and the believers had finished the military campaign of Dhat-Ar-Riqa, they stopped at a place to spend the night. The Messenger ﷺ chose guards from the Companions to take turns for night watch. Among them were Ammar ibn Yasir and Abbad ibn Bishr on one watch.

Abbad saw that his companion Ammar was exhausted, so he demanded that he sleep the first part of the night and he would stand guard so his companion could take some rest. He could resume guard after he awoke.

Abbad saw that the place around him was safe, so he thought, why not fill up his time with prayer, so that he would be rewarded both for praying and standing guard. So, he stood praying. While he was standing reciting a surah from the Quran after Al-Fatiha, an arrow passed through his shoulder, so he pulled it out and continued his prayer. Then the attacker shot a second arrow in the darkness of the night, so he pulled it out, also, and completed his recitation. Then he bowed and prostrated. Weakness and pain had dissipated his strength, so he extended his right hand, while prostrating, to his companion sleeping near him and continued to shake him until he woke up. Then he sat up from his prostration and recited the Tashahhud (the last part of his prayer) and completed his prayer.

Ammar awoke at the weary, trembling voice of his words, "Stand guard in my place. I am wounded!" Ammar jumped up yelling noisily and quickly frightened away the attackers, so they ran away. Then he turned to Abbad and said to him, "Glory be to Allah! Why didn't you awaken me when you were first hit?"

Abbad replied, "In my prayer I was reciting verses from the Quran that filled my soul with such awe that I didn't want to interrupt it nor cut it short. By Allah, I swear, because I did not want to lose a single word which the Messenger of Allah ordered me to preserve, I would have preferred death more than interrupting those verses which I was reciting." Abbad's love of Allah, His Messenger, and His religion was truly heartfelt, and this devotion lasted throughout his life.

Abbad once heard the Prophet ﷺ saying to the Ansar, "You are my people. You are the people who protect [I cannot be defeated through you]. There is no nation which has come like you before." Abbad certainly had the qualities that the Prophet described that day. He spent generously of his wealth and gave his life to the way of Allah and His Messenger. Worship completely absorbed him, bravery and heroism engrossed him, and generosity engaged him.

As a strong believer, he pledged his life to his faith and was well known for it by the other Companions. The Mother of the Faithful, Aisha said: "There are three from among the Ansar who are not surpassed in virtue by anyone: Sa'ad ibn Muad, Usaid ibn Hudair and Abbad ibn Bishr."

The first Muslims knew Abbad as a man radiant with Allah's light. His clear vision guided others to goodness and certainty. His brothers believed in his 'light' to the extent that they once agreed that Abbad was walking in the darkness when a light emanated from him that lit the way.

In the apostasy wars after the death of the Messenger ﷺ, Abbad took his role to defend Islam seriously, with death-defying courage. On the battlefield of Yamama, where the Muslims faced the most cruel and skilful army of Musailamah the Liar, Abbad's willingness to sacrifice was clear.

A day before the Battle began, Abbad saw in his sleep a somewhat unclear vision. We shall let the honourable companion, Abu Sa'id

Al-Khudri, tell us the story of this vision, and his incredible response which ended in martyrdom. Abu Sa'id reported: "Abbad ibn Bishr said to me, 'O Abu Sa'id, I saw last night as if the sky had opened up for me. Then it closed and covered over me. Indeed, I see it, if Allah wills, to mean martyrdom.' I said to him, Good. I swear by Allah, you did indeed see it.' On the Day of Yamama, I looked at him and indeed saw him shouting to the Ansar, 'Use your swords forcefully and be distinguished among the people!' So, 400 men came quickly to him, all of them from among the Ansar people, until they stopped at the gate of the garden. They fought violently, and Abbad ibn Bishr was martyred. I saw on his face much beating and I did not know him except by a mark that was on his body."

Thus, Abbad excelled in his duties as a believer from the Ansar. When Abbad had seen the destructive battle turning in favour of the enemy, he remembered the words of the Messenger to his people, the Ansar: "You are my people. You are the people who protect [I cannot be defeated through you]. There has not come any people like you before." These words filled his heart and soul, until it was as if the Messenger ﷺ was standing before him repeating those inspirational words directly to him.

It was then that Abbad called on the Ansar to be "honoured and distinguished" by fighting more valiantly for Allah's sake. When those 400 answered his call, he led them (along with Abu Dajanah and Al-Bara ibn Malik) to the 'garden of death', where Musailamah's army had fortified itself for protection. He truly honoured his oath of allegiance that day, and attained martyrdom. His vision in his dream the day before came true. Did he not see the sky open until, when he entered it from that opening, it returned and folded on him and closed?

He interpreted it as meaning that his spirit would ascend in the coming battle to its Creator. The vision and its interpretation proved true. And the doors of heaven were opened to welcome the spirit of Abbad ibn Bishr, the man bore a light from Allah within him.

(56)

SUHAIL IBN AMR

From Liberation to Martyrdom

When Suhail ibn Amr was captured by the Muslims during the Battle of Badr, Umar ibn Al-Khattab approached the Messenger of Allah ﷺ and said, "O Messenger of Allah, let me extract the teeth of Suhail ibn Amr until no speaker stands against you after today." The great Messenger responded, "No, Umar. I do not treat anyone harshly, so that Allah will not harm me, even though I am a Prophet." Then Umar came nearer and the Prophet said, "Perhaps Suhail will take a stand [one day] that will make you happy."

The prophecy of the Messenger came true. The greatest orator of the Quraysh, Suhail ibn Amr, transformed into a brilliant speaker for Islam. This polytheist who was always against Islam changed entirely into an obedient believer. Previously, he had been one of the senior chiefs of the Quraysh and a leader of its army. He was now a Muslim warrior who vowed persevere in his courage, self-control, and fighting in the way of Islam until he died on that path alone, so that perhaps Allah would forgive his previous sins.

Let us look to his early life. Suhail ibn Amr was one of the most prominent leaders of the Quraysh, and widely considered a man of intelligence and discernment. He was once appointed by the Quraysh to convince the Messenger to change his mind and refrain from entering Makkah in the year of Hudaibiyah. Let us consider this story in more detail.

At the end of 6 AH, the Messenger and his Companions went out to Makkah to visit the Sacred House and to perform Umrah. They did not want war and they were not prepared to fight. The Quraysh knew they were on their way to Makkah, so they went out to block their path and stop them from achieving their objective. The situation quickly escalated. The Messenger said to his Companions, "The Quraysh do not call me today to a plan but ask me instead about the bonds of kinship. So, I gave them to them."

The Quraysh began to send their messengers and representatives to the Prophet, so he informed all of them that he did not come to fight but to visit the Sacred House and glorify its sacredness. Each time one of their representatives returned, they sent another after him - more unyielding and stronger in persuasion - until they chose Urwah ibn Masud Ath-Thaqafi. He was among the strongest and cleverest of them. The Quraysh thought that Urwah would be able to convince the

Messenger to go back; however, he quickly came back to them saying, "O people of Quraysh, indeed I went to the Persian emperor in his kingdom and Caesar in his kingdom and the Negus in his kingdom, but, by Allah, I swear I never saw a king whose people magnify him as the Companions of Muhammad magnify him. I saw around him a people that shall never surrender to evil. So, what will you do and what is your opinion?"

At that time the Quraysh believed that there was no chance of success, so they decided to resort to negotiation and reconciliation. They chose for this task the most suitable of their chiefs, Suhail ibn Amr.

When the Muslims saw Suhail coming towards them, they recognised him immediately. They realised then that the Quraysh were resorting to diplomacy and peace making by sending Suhail. He sat down in front of the Messenger, and a long dialogue began that concluded with the drafting of a peace treaty. Suhail had tried to gain much for the Quraysh in their negotiations. The Prophet ﷺ had exercised tolerance, leniency, and noble-mindedness during the negotiations which helped Suhail to achieve much of that.

Two years passed, and the Quraysh violated the same treaty. The Messenger and the Muslims therefore began their conquest of Makkah. After a peaceful end to this conquest, the Muhajirun were finally able to return to their homes from which they had once been expelled by force. They returned and brought with them the Ansar, who had taken care of them in Medina and preferred their Makkan neighbours over themselves.

With the Muslim standards fluttering victoriously in the sky, Makkah opened all of its gates and the polytheists were struck by bewilderment. What would be their fate, after the years that they had spent killing, burning, torturing and starving the Muslims? The merciful Prophet ﷺ turned to them in a noble manner and said to them mercifully, "O people of Quraysh, what do you think I will do with you?"

Suhail ibn Amr, an enemy of Islam at the time, stepped forward and answered, "We think you will treat us well, O noble brother and son of a noble brother." A smile formed on the Prophet's lips and he called to them, "Go, you are free, liberated." These words sought to change the

Quraysh's feelings by guiding them towards humility and repentance. At the same moment, this response stimulated all of Suhail ibn Amr's feelings, and so he surrendered to Allah, the Lord of the Worlds. His Islam, at that time, was not the surrender of a defeated man, resigned to fate. It was, as his future shall reveal in what follows, the surrender of a man overwhelmed and fascinated by the majesty of Muhammad ﷺ, and the grandeur of his religion demonstrated in his conduct in conformity with its teachings. These teachings, as he saw them, conveyed extraordinary benevolence, friendship, and devotion.

Those who announced their Islam on the Day of the Conquest of Makkah were designated with the name 'At-Tulaqa' or those who were transferred by the forgiveness of the Prophet from polytheism to Islam when he said to them, "Go, you are free." Consequently, some persons from among those Tulaqa were raised by their sincerity to eventually become righteous and devoted Companions. Among these was Suhail ibn Amr.

Islam moulded and fashioned him afresh, refining all of his original skills and placing them at the service of truth, goodness, and faith. They once described Suhail in these words: "The kind, generous, outstanding one. The one who performs prayer much and fasts and gives in charity and reads the Quran and cries out of fear of Allah."

That was the greatness of Suhail. For in spite of the fact that he accepted Islam on the Day of the Conquest of Makkah, and not before that, we can see him truthfully affirming his Islam thereafter, with all his heart. He was completely transformed into a worshipper, self-denying and moderate, who constantly strove in the path of Allah and Islam.

When the Messenger ﷺ was transported to the company of the Most High, the news soon reached Makkah. Suhail was living there at that time, and the Muslims were overwhelmed by agitation, just as their brethren in Medina. However, the confusion of Medina was dissipated by Abu Bakr at that time by his decisive words: "Whoever worships Muhammad, know that Muhammad is dead; and whoever worships Allah, indeed Allah is living and never dies."

Suhail actually held the same position in Makkah as Abu Bakr in Medina. He gathered all of the Muslims there, and impressed on them the importance of this moment. He told them that Muhammad was truly the Messenger of Allah; that he did not die until he had executed his trust and conveyed the message; and that the duty of the believers towards this message was to devote all their efforts to it, using the Prophet's methodology.

On account of Suhail's position and his rightly guided words, he warded off any discord when the news of the death of the Messenger reached them. Did not he, the Messenger ﷺ, say to Umar that day at Badr (when Umar asked the Prophet for permission to pull out Suhail's two teeth)," [Leave them] Perhaps Suhail will take a stand [one day] that will make you happy"?

So, on the day when the news of Suhail's speech reached the Muslims in Medina, Umar ibn Al- Khattab remembered the prophecy of his Messenger and laughed a long time. For the day had truly come when Islam benefited from Suhail's front teeth, which Umar had wanted once to tear out.

When Suhail accepted Islam on the Day of the Conquest of Makkah and after he had tasted the sweetness of faith, he imposed on himself a vow he summed up in these words: "By Allah, I do not leave situations and battles with the polytheists except I support the Muslims equally and no wealth I spent with the polytheists but I spend an equal amount with the Muslims. Perhaps my support of the Muslims will be followed by an ever greater support, I stood a long time with the polytheists in front of their idols, so let us now stand for a long time with the believers in the presence of Allah, the One and Only."

Thus, he started praying and fasting continuously. He would not let a chance pass him by that would sharpen his spirit, but that he took from it a sufficient portion. In the past, he may have stood with the polytheists in the oppression of and the war against Islam. But, now he fought bravely with the Muslim army, he fought to extinguish the fire of others, including the Persian king who used to worship false gods other than Allah. He also fought to destroy the darkness of Rome's leaders, and to spread the word of monotheism and the greatness of Allah in every place he came across.

Suhail once went out with the Muslim army to Syria to participate in the wars there. On the Day of Yarmuk, the Muslims courageously plunged into battle, encountering harm, violence, and danger. Suhail ibn Amr eagerly stepped forward, hoping for a chance to wipe out the sins and mistakes of jahiliyya before accepting Islam.

He used to love his house in Makkah greatly, so much so that it made him forget himself. Nevertheless, he refused to return to it after the Muslim victory over Syria, and so he said, “I heard the Messenger of Allah saying, ‘The rank and position of one of you who spends one hour in the cause of Allah is better for him than his work throughout his life.’ Therefore, I will strive in the path of Allah until death, and I shall not return to Makkah.”

And Suhail died true to his vow. He continued to strive for the remainder of his life committed to his religion until the appointed time of his demise. So, his soul flew quickly to the Mercy of Allah and His pleasure.

(57)

ABU MUSA AL-ASHARI

Master of Horsemen

When Umar ibn Al-Khattab sent Abu Musa Al-Ashari to Basra to become its governor, he gathered its inhabitants and said, "Indeed the Commander of the Faithful Umar sent me to you to instruct you in the Book of your Lord and the traditions of your Prophet and to purify your ways for you."

The people were astonished. Never before had they realised that one of the incumbent duties of a commanding governor was to show them how to be people of culture and education. They were curious to see how he would purify their practices and give them a better understanding of their religion.

So, who was this ruler about whom it was once said: "No horseman ever came to Basra who was better for its people than him"? Indeed, he was Abdullah ibn Qais, nicknamed Abu Musa Al-Ashari.

He departed from his homeland of Yemen for Makkah immediately upon hearing of the appearance of a Messenger there; a Messenger who was calling to monotheism with clear vision and noble morals. In Makkah, he sat in the presence of the Messenger of Allah ﷺ and received guidance and certainty from his words. He then returned to his country carrying the word of Allah. Afterwards, he returned to the Messenger ﷺ immediately after the victory over Khaibar. His arrival coincided with the arrival of Jafar ibn Abu Talib, returning with his companions from Abyssinia, so the Messenger gave all of them a share of the booty.

On this occasion, Abu Musa did not come alone, but with approximately 50 men from the people of Yemen, including his two brothers Abu Ruhm and Abu Burdah, to whom the Messenger ﷺ also taught Islam. The Prophet named this delegation and its people the Ashariyin. He ﷺ described them as the people with the most delicate feelings and kind, gentle hearts. He also said of them: "If they exhausted their food in a military campaign or their food became diminished, they would gather what they possessed in one garment and divide it among themselves equally. So, they are from me and I am from them."

From that day, Abu Musa took his permanent and high place among the Muslims who were destined to be the Companions of the Messenger of Allah ﷺ. They were to become his pupils, and the carriers of Islam to the world in every age and time.

Abu Musa's character was a wonderful combination of extraordinary attributes. He was a bold and daring fighter, a firm combatant when he was forced to fight; while at the same time he was peaceful, kind and gentle almost to the extreme. He was a scholar who possessed comprehension, sound judgment, and judicious discernment. He was intelligent, and his understanding excelled in the most complicated and obscure issues It was said of him, "The judges of this nation are four: Umar, Ali, Abu Musa and Zaid ibn Thabit."

Whoever attempted to deceive Abu Musa in the matters of Allah, was himself deceived. He possessed great loyalty and earned the trust of the people.

In terms of jihad, Al-Ashari carried his responsibility with such heroism that the Prophet ﷺ would call him, "Master of horsemen, Abu Musa." We get an idea of his life as a warrior, from his own words when he described: "We went out with the Messenger of Allah on a military campaign… our feet were full of holes and my feet were also full of holes, until I lost my toenails and we wrapped our feet with rags." Such was his dedication and self-sacrifice on the battlefield.

His goodness and conviction were never provoked or exploited, not even by an enemy in battle. Even in wartime, he saw matters with complete clarity. For instance, when the Muslims were conquering Persia, Al-Ashari brought his army down upon the people of Isfahan. They agreed to pay him the jizya, so he made a peace settlement with them instead of fighting.

However, the Persians were not truthful in their agreement. They sought only to make themselves ready for a treacherous surprise attack. Nevertheless, the cleverness of Abu Musa was not oblivious to their secret plan. He perceived and saw through their scheme and the evil plans they were contriving, so when they began their attack, the leader was not taken by surprise. Therefore, the war overwhelmed the Persians, and within the day he gained a decisive victory.

In the battles against Imperial Persia, Abu Musa's performance was outstanding; his fighting for the cause of Allah was always noble. In the Battle of Tustar in particular, Abu Musa was again the hero. On that day, the Commander of the Faithful, Umar, supplied him with a massive number of Muslims, headed by Ammar ibn Yasir, Al-Bara ibn Malik, Anas ibn Malik, Majah Al-Bakri and Salamah ibn Raja. The two armies – both the Muslims under the command of Abu Musa and the Persians under the command of Hurmuzan - met in one of the fiercest and most ruthless battles of the time. The Persians withdrew inside the fortified city of Tustar and the Muslims besieged it for many days until Abu Musa intervened. He employed his skill and intelligence to send 200 cavalry men in with a Persian agent. Abu Musa instructed him to enter the fort in order to open the gate of the city, in front of an advanced guard that he personally chose for the mission. The gates had hardly opened when the soldiers of the advanced guard charged on the fortified citadel. Then, Abu Musa swooped down with his army to launch a large scale attack.

In just a few hours, he captured this crucial, fortified position, and the Persian leader surrendered. Abu Musa then sent them to Medina to hear the Commander of the Faithful's judgment on their future. Abu Musa though did not leave the battlefield for some time. Even after the Persians departed, he remained there crying to Allah and reciting the Quran in the sweetest of voices. He had a voice that made the inner heart of its listener tremble. The Messenger ﷺ once said about him, "Abu Musa was given a musical voice like the musical instruments of the people of Dawud." Every time Umar saw him he called him to recite to him from the Book of Allah saying to him, "Make us aspire to our Lord, O Abu Musa."

It should be noted that Abu Musa did not normally participate in fighting, except against armies who sought to extinguish the light of Allah. Whenever there was a fight between Muslims however, he avoided having any part in it whatsoever. This position of his was clear in the dispute between Ali and Muawiyah, as we shall see.

Perhaps this point, from the following account, will let us understand the most famous position of Abu Musa's life. That was his position in the arbitration between Imam Ali and Muawiyah. This position is often taken as evidence of either the immoderation in Abu Musa's good nature, or his naivety. However, the situation, as we shall see, reveals the greatness of his soul, and how much faith he had in the truth and in people.

In this arbitration, Abu Musa saw only that the Muslims were killing one another and each party fanatically clinging to its ruler. As he saw it, the situation between the combatants had reached a critical state that was impossible of resolve, and placed the destiny of the Muslim nation on the edge of an abyss.

The civil war, at that point, revolved around two Muslim parties, disputing over the person of the ruler. Some desired Imam Ali to relinquish the caliphate temporarily and Muawiyah to renounce it, so that the entire matter could be referred again to the Muslims. Then, they could choose, by way of consultation, the Caliph they wanted. This was how Abu Musa argued the case and this was the path that he saw to resolution.

It is correct that Imam Ali was soundly sworn in as Caliph, and correct that an illegal rebellion should not normally be allowed, simply to overturn a legally acquired caliphate. However, the issues in the dispute between Imam Ali and Muawiyah (and also between the peoples of Iraq and Syria) had, in the view of Abu Musa, reached a state which required a new kind of thinking and resolution. For the insurgency of Muawiyah was not considered just a revolt, and the rebellion of the Syrian people was not considered as just an insurrection, far from it. This discord was not just a difference in opinion. But, all these factors had developed into a harmful civil war. This had led to losses of thousands of people on both sides, and continued to threaten Islam with dire consequences. So, the removal of the causes of the dispute was, in Abu Musa's mind, the starting point on the road to salvation.

The view of Imam Ali, when he accepted the principle of arbitration, was that Abdullah ibn Abbas or someone from among his companions would represent him in arbitration. However, a large party of those with power in his group and army imposed Abu Musa Al-Ashari as his representative instead. The reason for their choice was that Abu Musa had never participated in the dispute between Ali and Muawiyah since it first began. He had separated himself from both parties after giving up all hope of encouraging the two of them to a common understanding and peace. From this respect, he had the most right of all people to arbitrate.

There was nothing in Abu Musa's religion or sincerity that made the Imam suspicious of him. But, Imam Ali did realise the muddied intentions of the other party, and the degree of their dependency on deception. He was concerned that Abu Musa, in spite of his understanding and knowledge, disliked such tactics and preferred to deal with people on the basis of truth, rather than wit. Therefore, Imam Ali was afraid Abu Musa would be deceived by Muawiyah's representative, and that the arbitration would be turned to favour one side, only making matters worse.

Nonetheless, the arbitration between the two parties began, with Abu Musa Al-Ashari representing the party of Imam Ali, and Amr ibn Al-As representing the party of Muawiyah. Amr ibn Al-As depended on his sharp wits and his broad cunning in carrying the banner for Muawiyah.

The meeting between the two men, Al-Ashari and Amr, began with a proposal presented by Abu Musa. It was for the two arbitrators to agree on the nomination of Abdullah ibn Umar as the caliph of the Muslims, because he enjoyed a broad consensus of admiration and distinction. Amr ibn Al-As however saw this as a great opportunity to persuade Abu Musa away from Imam Ali, and so he took advantage of it.

The content of the proposal by Abu Musa did not require a conditional link with the party which he represented, that of Imam Ali. As he had suggested Abdullah ibn Umar as an alternative for caliph, that meant to Amr that Abu Musa was ready to give support and backing for a caliph from others among the Prophet's Companions.

Thus, Amr found, by his shrewdness, an opening for the achievement of his goal. So, he therefore suggested Muawiyah. Then he suggested his own son Abdullah, who possessed a great position among the Messenger's Companions. The intelligence of Abu Musa was no less than Amr's wit however. When he saw Amr nominating in such a way, he boldly confronted Amr, saying that the choice of caliph was the right of all Muslims and that Allah had made their affair one of consultation between themselves. Thus, it was incumbent to leave the people alone to their right of choice.

We shall now see how Amr exploited even this lofty principle for the interest of Muawiyah. However, before that, let us listen to the historical dialogue which took place between Abu Musa and Amr ibn Al-As at the beginning of their meeting. We transmit it on the authority of the book Al-Akhbar At-Tawal by Abu Hunaifah Ad-Daiyanuri.

Abu Musa: "O Amr, do you desire in this matter the good of the nation and the pleasure of Allah?"

Amr: "And what is it?"

Abu Musa: "That we appoint Abdullah ibn Umar, for indeed he never involved himself in the war."

Amr: "And where are you with respect to Muawiyah?"

Abu Musa: "Muawiyah does not deserve it, nor is he worthy of it."

Amr: "Do you not know that Uthman was unjustly killed?"

Abu Musa: "Yes."

Amr: "So, indeed Muawiyah is guardian (wali) of the blood of Uthman and his house is in the Quraysh, as you know. So, the people said, 'Why not assume responsibility for the matter since it has no precedents. In that you have no excuse. You say, I indeed found him the guardian of Uthman's blood and Allah Most High says, *And whoever is killed (intentionally with hostility and oppression and not by mistake), We have given his heir the authority* (17:33).' The brother of Umm Habiba, the wife of the Prophet ﷺ has this [view] and he is one of his Companions.

Abu Musa: "Fear Allah, O Amr! As for what you mentioned concerning the nobility of Muawiyah, if worthiness for the caliphate were based on nobility, the one with the most right to it among the people would be Abrahah ibn As-Sabbah, for indeed he is one of the sons in the line of the kings of Yemen, who ruled the east of the earth and its west. Furthermore, how does the nobility of Muawiyah compare with that of Ali ibn Abu Talib? As for your talk that Muawiyah was the guardian of Uthman's blood, his son Amr ibn Uthman is more Uthman's guardian than he. But if you acceded to me, we would revive the practice of Umar ibn Al-Khattab and his son Abdullah."

Amr: "What prevents you from my son, Abdullah, with his merit and goodness and his previous hijra and his companionship?"

Abu Musa: "Indeed your son is a truthful man, but you have completely immersed him into these wars…"

Amr: "O Abu Musa, no man is suitable for this affair unless he has two molars. He eats with one and he feeds (others) with the other."

Abu Musa: "Woe to you, O Amr! Indeed, the Muslims have entrusted the matter to us, after they have fought with one another by force of arms and swords. Do not hurt them with spears! Do not turn them back to civil war and discord."

Amr: "So what do you see?"

Abu Musa: "I see that we should depose the two men, Ali and Muawiyah. Then make consultation between the Muslims. They will choose for themselves who they want."

Amr: "I am pleased with this view. So, indeed the goodness of the heart is in it. This argument completely changes the form which we are accustomed to see."

Indeed, in these arguments Abu Musa was not negligent, but proactive. Contrary to what was expected of him, he exercised his intelligence more than Amr ibn Al-As, who was famous for his shrewdness. So, when Amr wanted to propose the caliphate of Muawiyah based on genealogy in the Quraysh and guardianship of the blood of Uthman, Abu Musa's refusal came as sharply as the edge of a sword.

After this exchange, the responsibility for what followed was assumed by Amr ibn Al-As alone. Abu Musa is exonerated from guilt, as he chose to refer the matter back to the nation to choose their caliph democratically. Amr appeared to agree and adhere to this view. It did not come to Abu Musa's mind that Amr would threaten Islam by resorting to more cunning manoeuvres, regardless of his conviction about Muawiyah. When Abu Musa returned to his party and informed them about his conversation with Amr, Ibn Abbas warned Abu Musa, "By Allah I fear that Amr will trick you, so if the two of you agree on something, let him come forward before you to speak. Then you speak after him."

However, Abu Musa saw the situation on a higher level than pure tactics. From then on, he had no doubt of Amr's commitment to their agreement. Therefore, they gathered the following day, with Abu Musa representing Imam Ali and Amr ibn Al-As representing Muawiyah. Abu Musa invited Amr to speak first, but Amr refused and said to him, "I am not going to precede you when you are more virtuous than I, and emigrated before me, and are older than me."

So, Abu Musa advanced first and greeted the waiting crowd from both parties. He said, "O people, indeed, in this matter concerning which Allah has gathered together this nation and to put its affair in proper order, we do not see anything better than the deposition of the two men, Ali and Muawiyah and to call for consultation among the people to choose for themselves whom they like. Therefore, I depose Ali and Muawiyah. So, take upon yourselves as guardians whom you love."

Now, the turn of Amr ibn Al-As came to announce the deposition of Muawiyah, just as Abu Musa had deposed Ali, in fulfilment of the confirmed, established agreement of the previous day.

Amr ascended the pulpit and said, "O people, indeed, Abu Musa has said what you heard and deposed his companion. Indeed, I depose his companion just as he deposed him and confirm my companion Muawiyah. He is indeed, the guardian of the Commander of the Faithful, Uthman, and the guardian of his blood, and the one having the most right to his dignified position."

Shocked, Abu Musa did not conceive this outcome possible, and he reprimanded Amr severely with furious words. Disappointed that nothing more could come of the arbitration, he returned again to his seclusion and made his way swiftly back to Makkah. Close to the House of Allah, he spent the remainder of his days there.

From all this, we see that Abu Musa (may Allah be pleased with him) had a position of trust and love with the Messenger ﷺ, and a position of trust with his Companions and successors. In his life the Prophet gave him, along with Muad ibn Jabal, the governorship over Yemen. After the death of the Messenger, he returned to Medina to carry out his responsibility in the great holy war between the Muslim, Persian and Roman armies.

In the period of Umar, the Commander of the Faithful, Abu Musa was governor of Basra, and Caliph Uthman put him in charge of Kufa. He was one of the people of the Quran, those who memorised it, understood it, and acted on it. Some of his radiant words about the Quran were "Follow the Quran and do not desire that the Quran should follow you."

Abu Musa was truly persistent in his worship and on the hardest days for fasting, he would cherish the fast and say, "Perhaps the thirst of the midday heat will be intercession for us on the Day of Judgment." On one such humid day, Abu Musa's appointed time of death came to him. It covered his countenance with a radiance reserved only for those who hope in the mercy of Allah and a good reward. And the words which he oft repeated during his faithful life, tripped off his tongue in his parting moments: "O Allah, You are peace and from You is peace."

(58)

AT-TUFAIL IBN AMR AD-DAWSI

The Rightly Guided Nature

In the land of Daws, At-Tufail grew up in a noble and respected family. He was gifted with the art of poetry, and his fame spread among the tribes. During the season of Ukadh, when Arab poets came from all directions and people gathered to hear them to show off their skills, At-Tufail would take his place in the forefront.

He also used to frequent Makkah at times other than Ukadh. Once, he visited Makkah when the Messenger ﷺ had just started declaring his mission. The Quraysh feared that At-Tufail would meet him, convert to Islam, and then put his poetic gift at the service of Islam. That would be a curse upon the Quraysh and their idols. On account of this, they instead surrounded him with every kind of hospitality and comfort during his visit. They then went on to warn him about meeting the Messenger of Allah. One of the Quraysh said to him, "He has charming speech like magic and he makes division between a man and his son, and a man and his brother, and a man and his wife. I fear for you and your people from him. So do not talk to him nor listen to any talk from him."

Let us listen to At-Tufail himself telling the remainder of the story: "So by Allah, they were still insisting on my not listening to anything from him and not meeting him. And when I went over to the Kaba, I filled my ears with cotton so as not to hear anything he had to say when he spoke. There I found him standing praying at the Kaba, so I stood close to him. Allah refused nothing but He made me hear some portion of what he was reading. I heard a fine speech, and I said to myself…'Indeed, I am an intelligent poet. I would not fail to recognise the good from the ugly. What is it that hinders me from listening to the man and what he says? If that which he brings is good, I should accept it, and if it is bad...'

'I stayed until Muhammad departed to his house. I followed him until he entered his house, so I entered behind him and said to him, 'O Muhammad, verily your people have told me such-and-such about you. By Allah, they kept making me afraid of you until I blocked my ears with cotton in order not to hear your words. But Allah willed that I hear, so I heard a fine speech. Set forth to me your message.

'So the Messenger presented to me Islam and recited to me from the Quran. By Allah, I had never heard a speech better than it, nor a matter more just than it. So, I surrendered and bore witness to the truth. I said, 'O Messenger of Allah, indeed I am a person of credibility among my people and I am returning to them to invite them to Islam, so call on Allah to make a sign for me that will be a help for me in that which I call them to'. He said, 'O Allah, make for him a sign'."

Allah has spoken of the value of listening in His book: *Those who listen to the speech and follow the best part of it* (39:18). Surely At-Tufail was of these people, as no sooner had he heard the Quran, than he accepted the message of Islam. He stretched out his right hand to swear the oath of allegiance, heart fully open. Not only that, but he immediately took upon himself the responsibility of inviting his people and kin to this religion of truth and the straight path.

For this reason, as soon as he reached his country and house in the land of Daws, he confronted his father about the principles of faith and perseverance. He called his father to Islam after telling him of the Messenger's call. He spoke to him about his greatness, purity and honesty, and his father became a Muslim immediately. Then he went to his mother, and she became a Muslim. Then to his wife, and she became a Muslim. When he was sure that Islam had swept over his whole household, he moved on to his tribe and to all the inhabitants of Daws. However, no one from among them accepted Islam except Abu Hurairah (may Allah be pleased with him).

They went on disappointing him and turning away from him until he ran out of patience with them. So, At-Tufail rode his mount through the desert, returning to the Messenger of Allah in order to complain and to learn more from him. When he arrived in Makkah, he hastened to the house of the Messenger, driven by his yearning to see him. He said to the Prophet ﷺ, "O Messenger of Allah, indeed adultery and usury have beaten me in our fight over Daws. So, call on Allah to destroy Daws." Suddenly, At-Tufail was baffled when he saw the Messenger raise his hands to the sky while saying, "O Allah, guide Daws and bring them to Islam as Muslims." Then he turned to At-Tufail and said to him, "Return to your people, call them and be lenient with them."

This moment filled the soul of At-Tufail with awe, and filled his spirit with peace. He thanked Allah deeply for making this merciful Messenger his teacher, and for making Islam his religion. He returned to his people, and there he went on calling to Islam but more leniently, just as the Messenger had advised him.

During the period he spent among his people, the Messenger emigrated to Medina and the battles of Badr, Uhud and Khandaq took place. While the Messenger of Allah was in Khaibar, after Allah had given the Muslims victory over it, a full procession including 80 families from Daws approached the Messenger saying, "There is no god but Allah and Allah is the Greatest." They sat before him giving the oath of allegiance one after the other.

When this remarkable spectacle came to an end, At-Tufail ibn Amr sat by himself, recalling his steps that had brought him to this blessed moment. He remembered the day he came to the Messenger asking him to raise his hands to the sky saying, "O Allah, destroy Daws" and the Prophet instead supplicated for their guidance. Allah had indeed guided Daws and brought them together as Muslims. And here they were, 80 families (the majority of its inhabitants), taking their place in the pure ranks behind the trustworthy Messenger of Allah.

At-Tufail continued his work with the believing community, and on the day of the Conquest of Makkah, he entered it with tens of thousands of Muslims. He saw that day, the Messenger of Allah destroying the idols of the Kaba and purifying it with his own hands. Immediately afterwards, he remembered an idol belonging to Amr ibn Humamah. Whenever he stayed over as his guest, he used to show it to him, so he became fearful in its presence and even pleaded to it. Now the opportunity had come for At-Tufail to erase the sin of those days from his soul. He approached the Messenger, requesting permission to go burn the idol of Humamah called 'The Two Palms', and the Prophet ﷺ gave him permission.

At-Tufail went over and lit the fire on it and every time the flame went down, he stoked it again to a blazing fire. All the while he said,

O Idol of Two Palms,
I am not one of your worshippers.
Our origin is older than your origin.
I have filled fire in your heart.

It was in this way that At-Tufail lived with the Prophet ﷺ, praying behind him, learning from him, and fighting with him. Even after the Prophet's death, At-Tufail saw that his responsibility as a Muslim did not end there, but rather only just began. Therefore, no sooner had the apostasy wars erupted, than At-Tufail prepared for them. He embarked courageously on their hardships, yearning for martyrdom all the while.

In the Battle of Yamama, he went out with the Muslims accompanied by his son, Amr ibn At-Tufail. At the beginning of the battle he advised his son to fight the army of Musailamah the Liar, like one who desires death and martyrdom. He told him that he felt he would die in this battle, and thus his sword carried him. He plunged into the fight gloriously. He did not defend his life with his sword, but he defended his sword with his life.

In the battle, At-Tufail Ad-Dawsi was martyred. His body fell under a flurry of strikes as he waved farewell to his son, who was unable to see him amidst the crowd. He was waving to him as if calling him to join him. And he did in fact follow him, after only a short while. In the Battle of Yarmuk in Syria, Amr ibn At-Tufail went out to fight and also returned as a martyr. As his spirit came out of his breast, he extended his right hand as if to shake another's hand. And who knows? Perhaps at that time he was shaking hands with the spirit of his father, At-Tufail.

(59)

AMR IBN AL-AS

Liberator of Egypt

There were three from among the Quraysh who would trouble the Prophet ﷺ with the fierceness of their resistance to his call, and in their torture of his Companions. The Messenger called to them and pleaded to his Lord to inflict them with His punishment, and while he was doing this, he received the revelation of these noble verses: *The matter is not in your hands, whether God turns to them or chastises them, for surely they are evildoers.* (3:128)

The Messenger's understanding of the verse was that he was to stop calling Allah to punish them and to leave their affair to Allah alone. Either they would continue their wrongdoing and His punishment would be inflicted upon them, or He would accept their repentance.

They finally repented, so it was that Allah's infinite mercy reached them. Amr ibn Al-As was one of these three. Allah had chosen the path of repentance for all of them, so He guided them to Islam. He transformed Amr ibn Al-As into a Muslim warrior and into one of the bravest leaders of Islam.

In spite of some of Amr's discordant opinions, he was a glorious Companion. He sacrificed and gave generously; he was a defender and combatant, and in Egypt especially he is held in high esteem. We have Amr to thank for the introduction of Islam to Egypt and the guidance of Egypt to Islam. So, blessed is the gift and blessed is the gift giver.

The historians were accustomed to describe Amr as the conqueror of Egypt. However, this description is something of an underestimation and also an overestimation. Perhaps a more truthful description of Amr would be to call him the 'Liberator of Egypt'. For Islam did not conquer the country in the modern understanding of 'conquer', but it liberated it from the hegemony of two imperial powers. It set it free from the imperial powers of Persia and Rome.

Egypt had been plundered by the Romans, and its inhabitants had been resisting, all to no avail. When the call of Muslim armies sounded out, "Allahu akbar" they hastened together and embraced their arrival, seeking liberation from Caesar, and from Rome.

So, Amr and his men did not quite conquer Egypt, but they opened the way for Egypt to tie its destiny to the principles of truth and justice, in the light of Islamic principles. Amr was careful to keep the inhabitants of Egypt and its Copts away from the army. He restricted the fighting between himself and the occupying Romans who robbed the land and wealth from its people.

On account of that, we find a record of him speaking with the Christian leaders and their high priest. He said to them, "Indeed, Allah sent Muhammad with the truth and ordered him to teach it. The Prophet carried out his mission, and he died after leaving us on that path, the clear straight path. Among the things he ordered us to do was to be responsible to the people, so we call you to Islam. Whoever responds is of us. He has what we have and he has the same rights and obligations as we do. And whoever does not respond to Islam, we enforce on him the payment of jizya, and (in return) we offer to him defence and protection. Our Prophet informed us that Egypt would open for us and advised us to be good to its people, saying, 'Egypt will be opened to you after me, so you are advised to treat its Copts well, for indeed, they have a covenant of protection and kinship relations,' so if you answer to what we call you to, you will have protection and security."

No sooner had Amr finished his words, than some of the priests and rabbis shouted, saying, "Indeed the kinship of which your Prophet advised you is a remote kinship relationship, the like of which cannot be reached except by the prophets." In spite of what the Roman leader had tried to do to frustrate it, this was a good start for the relationship between Amr and the Egyptian Copts.

Amr ibn Al-As was not one of the early converts to Islam. He embraced Islam with Khalid ibn Al-Walid, just shortly before the Conquest of Makkah. Surprisingly, his Islam began at the hands of the King, An-Najashi, in Abyssinia.

An-Najashi knew Amr and respected him well, because of his several visits to Abyssinia, and the abundance of gifts he used to bring with him. In Amr's final visit to that country, mention was made of the Prophet who was calling to monotheism and to the nobility of morals in the Arabian Peninsula. The Abyssinian ruler asked Amr, "How could you not believe in him and follow him, when he is truly a Messenger from Allah?" Amr then asked An-Najashi, "Is he thus?" An-Najashi answered, "Yes, so obey me, O Amr, and follow him, for indeed, by Allah, he is on the path of truth and he will surpass those who stood against him!"

Struck by his words, Amr travelled by sea and immediately returned to his home country. There, he turned his face in the direction of Medina to surrender to Allah, Lord of the Worlds.

On the road leading to Medina, he met Khalid ibn Al-Walid coming from Makkah, also going to the Messenger ﷺ to swear allegiance to Islam. No sooner did the Messenger see the two of them coming, than his face beamed with joy and he said to his Companions, "Makkah has gifted you with its most noble leaders." Khalid approached and swore allegiance. Then Amr approached and said, "Indeed, I swear allegiance to you, provided that you ask Allah to forgive me my previous sins." So, the Messenger answered him saying, "O Amr, swear allegiance, for indeed Islam disregards whatever preceded it."

Amr swore allegiance and placed his wits and bravery at the service of his new religion. When the Messenger returned to Allah, Most Exalted, Amr was appointed ruler over Oman. During the caliphate of Umar he performed famously in the Syrian wars, and it was then that he went to liberate Egypt from the rule of Rome.

If only Amr ibn Al-As could have resisted the love of command, then he would have greatly overcome some of the positions which this entangled him in. However, Amr's love for ruling, was a direct expression of his nature, brimming with talent. Even his way of walking and talking implied that he was created for command. It is related that the Commander of the Faithful, Umar ibn Al-Khattab, once saw Amr approaching when he smiled and remarked, "It should not be for Abu Abdullah to walk on the earth except as a commander."

Even when dangerous events overwhelmed the Muslims, Amr dealt with these events in a commanding manner, as one who possesses intelligence, wits, and a confidently reassured capability. Moreover, he possessed such a portion of honesty that it made Umar ibn Al-Khattab (even though he was strict in choosing his governors) choose Amr as governor over Palestine and Jordan, then over Egypt. This, even though Umar knew that Amr had exceeded a certain limit imposed by his caliphate on the opulence of his life style.

So, despite the fact that Umar of Amr's abundant wealth, he did not remove him. Instead, he sent Muhammad ibn Maslamah to him and ordered Amr to split all of his wealth and possessions with him. So, he left him one half of it and carried the other half to the treasury in Medina. However, if the Commander of the Faithful had known that Amr's love for wealth would lead him to carelessness in his responsibility, it is conceivable that his reasonable conscience would not have allowed him to stay in power one moment longer.

Amr (may Allah be pleased with him) was sharp-witted, with a strong and intuitive foresight. This was so much so that whenever the Commander of the Faithful saw a person incapable of artifice, he clapped his palms in astonishment and said, "Glory be to Allah ! Indeed, the Creator of this and the Creator of Amr ibn Al-As is one God!"

Amr was also very daring and unhesitant. He would sometimes combine his daring with his wits to appear cowardly or hesitant. However, this was simply his capacity to trick - perfected with great skill - to get himself out of a destructive situation.

Caliph Umar knew these talents of his and appreciated their true value. For that reason, when he sent him to Syria, before his going to Egypt, it was said to the Commander of the Faithful, "At the head of the armies of Rome in Syria is Artubun, a shrewd and brave leader and a prince." Umar's response was, "We have hurled at Artubun of Rome, the Artubun of the Arabs, so let us see how the matter unfolds."

Matters unfolded in an overwhelming victory for the Artubun of the Arabs - their dangerous weapon, Amr ibn Al-As. He toppled the Artubun of Rome, who left his army to defeat and fled to Egypt. Amr would soon catch up with him to raise the standard of Islam above its Egyptian soil as well.

Amr's intelligence and wit excelled in many situations. However, we certainly do not count among them his stance in the arbitration with Abu Musa Al-Ashari. When the two of them privately agreed to depose Ali and Muawiyah, Abu Musa upheld his part of the agreement, while Amr failed to do so.

Instead, we find examples of Amr's true skill during his time as commander in the war with the Romans in Egypt, particularly at the

Citadel of Babylon (near present day Cairo). We also see the power of his intuition at the Battle of Yarmuk with the aforementioned Roman leader, Artubun. When Artubun and his commander invited Amr for talks, they deceitfully gave orders to some of their men to attack and kill him with rocks upon his departure from the citadel.

Amr met with the commander, not suspecting anything from him, and their meeting came to an end. While Amr was on his way out of the citadel though, he glimpsed over the walls something suspicious that sparked concern. He cleverly turned back to the commander, and with calm, slow steps, he acted as if nothing had aroused his suspicion. He met the commander again and said to him, "An idea came across my mind, I wanted you to know. I have with me, where my companions are camped, a group from among the first Companions of the Messenger to enter into Islam. The Commander of the Faithful would not decide anything without consulting them and would not send an army unless he put them at the head of its fighters and soldiers. I will bring them to you so that they hear from you that which I heard, so they will become as clear in the matter as I am."

The Roman commander believed that Amr had naively granted him the opportunity of a lifetime. Therefore, he thought it better to agree with him, so that when he returned with his commanders, and the best of their men, they would deliver the coup de grace. He aimed to finish them all off at once, instead of assassinating Amr alone. So, he secretly gave his order to put off Amr's murder and he saw Amr off cordially, shaking hands with enthusiasm as he left. Amr smiled the most intelligent of Arab smiles as he was leaving the Citadel. In the morning, Amr returned to the Citadel at the head of an army, mounted on his horse that whinnied almost in a loud burst of laughter. It, too, knew the shrewdness of its owner.

In 43 AH, death caught up with Amr ibn Al-As in Egypt, where he was ruling. He recaptured his life in the moments of departure, saying, "In the first part of my life I was a disbeliever, and I was one of the fiercest people against the Messenger of Allah, so if I had died on that day, the fire would have been my fate. Then, I swore allegiance to the Messenger of Allah, and there was no person more dear to me than he, nor more glorious in my eyes than he. If I wanted to describe him, I could not, because I was not able to fill my eyes with him, on account of being so in awe of him. If I had died back then, I would have wished to be of the inhabitants of Paradise. Then after that I was tested with command and with material things. I do not know if they were for me or against me."

Then he raised his reverent eyes to the skies, calling upon his Lord: "O Allah, I am not innocent, so forgive me. I am not mighty, so help me. And if Your mercy does not come to me, I will surely be of those destroyed." He continued in his prayers until his spirit ascended to Allah. His final words were, "There is no god but Allah."

Above his grave in Egypt, his seat still stands throughout the centuries. This seat was where he used to teach and adjudicate, beneath the ceiling of his ancient mosque, the Mosque of Amr. This was the first mosque in Egypt, in which the name of Allah, the One and Only was declared from its walls to its pulpit.

(60)

SALIM MAWLA ABU HUDHAIFAH

Blessed Be the Carrier of the Quran

The Messenger of Allah ﷺ advised his Companions one day, "Take the Quran from four people: Abdullah ibn Masud, Salim Mawla Abu Hudhaifah, Ubaiy ibn Kab and Muad ibn Jabal."

We have met before with Ibn Masud, Ubaiy and Muad. So, who was this fourth Companion whom the Messenger made an authority for teaching the Quran? He was Salim Mawla Abu Hudhaifah, named thus because he had been a slave once who had been emancipated and adopted by the great Abu Hudhaifah ibn Utbah. When Islam later abrogated the practice of adoption, Abu Hudhaifah became a brother, friend, and protector of those whom he had adopted. By the grace of Allah, Salim reached an elevated position which his virtues, behaviour and his piety had all prepared him for.

Abu Hudhaifah ibn Utbah became Muslim himself at an early age and hastened to Islam, leaving his father, Utbah ibn Rabufa, wallowing in anger. Utbah was largely concerned with the disruption that his son's conversion brough to his own life, as he was a noble among his people. His father had been preparing Abu Hudhaifah for leadership among the Quraysh.

But, Abu Hudhaifah had a higher calling. He freed and adopted Salim, they both continuously worshipped their Lord and were extremely patient under the hardship of the Quraysh. When the verses of the Quran were revealed which outlawed the practice of adoption, every adopted person returned to carrying the name of their biological father. So, Zaid ibn Haritha, for example, whom the Prophet had adopted - and who had been known among the Muslims as Zaid ibn Muhammad - became Zaid ibn Haritha. But Salim's father was not known to him, so Abu Hudhaifah became his guardian and he was called Salim 'Mawla' Abu Hudhaifah, meaning he was under his protection.

By cancelling the practice of adoption, perhaps Islam wanted to say to the Muslims: "Do not take kinship, nor the bond by which you affirm your brotherhood, as stronger than Islam itself, and the religious faith by which you are truly made brothers." The early Muslims understood this very well. So, nothing was more loved to any one of them after Allah and His Messenger than their brethren in faith.

We have seen how the Ansar welcomed their brethren, the Muhajirun. They shared with them their wealth, their homes, and all they owned. This too is what happened between Abu Hudhaifah, the noble of the Quraysh, and Salim. They remained more than brothers up to the last moment of their lives, even until death: they died together, close in spirit and in body.

Salim believed in Islam sincerely and took his path to Allah by adopting the behaviour of the devout. Neither his genealogy, nor his position in society had any consideration for him. He was elevated by his piety alone to the highest degree in Islam's new society. The faith had come to establish a more just foundation for that society, as summarised in the following glorious verse: *Surely, the most honourable of you in the sight of God is the most pious of you* (49:13) and in the noble hadiths: "Arabs have no superiority over non-Arabs except in piety", and "The son of a white woman has no superiority over the son of a black woman, except in piety."

In this rightly-guided society, Salim's protector, Abu Hudhaifah, found that he was afforded the privilege of government. Moreover, he found honour for his family, and was able to marry Salim to his niece Fatimah bint Al-Walid ibn Utbah. And in this new society, which destroyed the unjust class structure, Salim always found himself in the first rank on account of his truthfulness, faith, and bravery.

Salim even became an imam for the Muhajirun during their prayer in the Quba Mosque on the road to Medina. There is proof of this in the Book of Allah, when the Prophet ﷺ ordered the Muslims to learn from him. Alongside Salim were men of excellence, which made the Messenger remark, "Praise be to Allah, Who made in my nation the like of you." His Muslim brothers called him "Salim, from among the Righteous."

The story of Salim is much like the story of Bilal. It is the story of many poor people and slaves who were freed by Islam from the shackles of servitude and weakness. The new faith made the same people imams and commanders, in a society based entirely on knowledge, reason and integrity of conduct.

Salim had all the rightly guided virtues of Islam. Among his most prominent virtues was his overt, public frankness about what he perceived as the truth. He never stayed silent if he felt it was his duty to speak about something. For instance, after Makkah was liberated by the Muslims, the Prophet ﷺ sent some detachments to the villages and tribes around the city. These detachments were instructed to announce that they were coming only as callers to the faith, and so they were not there to harm them in any way.

At the head of one of these companies was Khalid ibn Al-Walid. When Khalid reached his destination, an incident led to him using his sword and blood was shed. When the Prophet ﷺ heard the news of these events, he apologised to his Lord for some time saying, "O Allah, indeed I absolve myself from all that Khalid has done." The Commander of the Faithful, Umar would often recall this incident and said of him, "In the sword of Khalid, indeed, is a heavy burden."

Salim Mawla Abu Hudhaifah had accompanied Khalid on this expedition, along with some other Companions. As soon as Salim witnessed Khalid's actions, he confronted him with a sharp objection. Salim went on to list the mistakes Khalid had committed. Khalid, the leader and war hero in both jahiliyya and Islam, listened for the first time, defended himself the second time, and became more forceful in his own speech the third time. All the while, Salim held fast to his point of view, and spoke without fear.

Salim was a slave not long before, but still he did not look at Khalid as a nobleman of Makkah. No, Islam had created equality between them. He did not look at him as a leader, venerating his errors, but as a partner in their responsibility towards Islam. Moreover, his opposition to Khalid did not originate from a selfish purpose; it was advice, consecrated by Islam, which was his right to bestow. What Salim heard all the time from his Prophet was, "Religion is sincere advice. Religion is sincere advice. Religion is sincere advice." And so, Salim acted on this principle.

When news of Khalid's actions reached the Messenger ﷺ, he asked, "Did anyone stand up to him?" His anger was pacified when they said to him, "Yes, Salim critically examined him and opposed him." This was Salim. He lived with his Messenger and the believers. He did not stay behind from any battle, nor did he refrain from performing any worship. And his brotherliness with Abu Hudhaifah only increased daily with both of them showing mutual self-sacrifice and solidarity.

After the Messenger ﷺ passed away, the caliphate of Abu Bakr was confronted with apostate conspiracies. Then, the Battle of Yamama came with its terrible war. Islam had not gone through anything like it before. Salim and Abu Hudhaifah went out to fight in the cause of Allah. At the start of the battle, the Muslims did not withstand the attack. However, each believer there felt that the battle was his own, and soon Khalid ibn Al-Walid reorganised the army with astonishing skill.

The brothers, Abu Hudhaifah and Salim, embraced the prospect of martyrdom for the sake of a religion of truth that had given them both the happiness of this world and the hope for the next. They threw themselves into the vast sea of battle. Abu Hudhaifah was calling, "O people of the Quran, decorate the Quran with your actions," and his sword tore through the battlefield like a hurricane against the army of Musailamah the Liar. Salim too was shouting, "What a bad carrier of the Quran I would be if the Muslims were attacked through me."

While Salim's sword was forceful on his enemies' necks, the swords of apostasy fell heavy upon him, cutting his right hand off as it carried the standard of the Muhajirun. This, after its bearer, Zaid ibn Al-Khattab, had already fallen. When his right hand was severed, he picked up the standard with his left and kept on waving it high while shouting the following noble Quranic verses: "*And how many of the Prophets have fought, and with them large troops of godly people? But they never lost heart when adversity befell them in God's cause, nor did they weaken, nor did they fail And God loves those who show fortitude.*" (3:146)

This most magnificent slogan was the one he chose on the day of his death. Shortly after, a group of apostates encircled Salim, and the hero fell. He managed to stay alive though to see the battle end with the killing of Musailamah the Liar, the defeat of his army, and the triumph of the Muslim army.

When the Muslims were examining their martyrs, they found Salim in the last pains of death. He asked them, "What has Abu Hudhaifah done?" They said, "He died a martyr." He said, "Lay me be next to him." They said, "He is next to you, O Salim." He had already died a martyr in the same place as his brother.

Salim smiled his last smile and did not speak again. He and his companion had realised what they had always desired. Together they had become Muslims. Together they had lived, and together they had died as martyrs.

And so, Salim returned to Allah, that great believer whom Umar ibn Al- Khattab spoke of on his own deathbed: "If Salim were alive, I would have given him the command after me."

FAREWELL

While we bid farewell to the graceful company of the Companions of the Prophet Muhammad (may peace and blessings be upon him and upon them all), we may ask ourselves, have we taken into account all of those great men? The answer is, quite simply, no. We have been honoured to closely examine a blessed number of them, but we were not fortunate enough to accompany all the Companions.

Indeed, the 60 men introduced in this book represent many thousands of others who saw the Messenger ﷺ, lived during his time, believed in him, and struggled with him. In the lives of these 60 righteous men though, we perceive an image of all the Companions. We see their faith, their steadfastness, their heroism, their sacrifices, and their loyalty. I desire not to repeat what I have already written about the amazing faith which filled the hearts of these men. But, we recognise all of their efforts and the victories they achieved in the name of Islam.

These 60 men then, are a superb example to us all. These heroes lived through a great age of human struggle and of especial religious struggle. It was an age when the ancient world was overtaken by a new force of truth. A truth which came to announce the oneness of Allah and the unity of His creation. There were no idols in this new era, no deified emperors or czars. It recognised that there is only One God Who is Allah, and all His people are as equal in His eyes as the teeth of a comb.

Muhammad ﷺ with his truth, steadfastness, purity, and eminence could not but reflect a rare quality of faith on the people around him. It was the faith of people who had known him well and had seen him in all his grace. They saw his humanity and his devotion to Allah; his loftiness and modesty; his superb qualities and his simplicity; his strength and his compassion.

They observed him, understood his noble motives, and mimicked his undeviating methods. Therefore, no doubt could prevent them from believing in him. Every nation has asked its prophet for a miracle in order to believe in him, all except Muhammad's Companions, the men around the Prophet ﷺ. They never said, "Show us a miracle as proof of your truthfulness." This was because Muhammad himself was the miracle. Seeking another miracle outside of him, his personality, and his principles would have been a kind of naivety. Their hearts had instead been filled with the guidance of Allah, and their perceptions had been illuminated with His light.

The faith of that first generation of Muslims instigated a revival of humanity, with its different religions, different ages and races. Before Islam, they were merely scattered, discordant tribes led by inflexible narrow-minded individuality. As a political power, they had not achieved anything of note. And, as an economic power, they were the poorest of people.

So, how did these minorities become the architects of a new world? Was it the power of weapons and the plenitude of armies? Surely not. Alexander before them and Genghis Khan after them had plenty of weapons and soldiers. Where is Alexander today? Where is Genghis Khan? What is left of them and their astounding victories? What is left of all that, in the conscience of mankind? Nothing.

Therefore, materialistic power was not the reason that turned the Companions of the Messenger ﷺ into what we have seen here. It was only faith; faith in the truth and in what is good. Above that, faith in the Lord of truth and good. This is the true lesson taught by Muhammad, the Messenger of Allah (may Allah be pleased with him and his Companions).

When people devote their lives to benefaction, surely darkness turns into light, chaos into order, and weakness into strength. In this pursuit of truth, property becomes protected, humiliation becomes greatness, privation becomes plenitude, and ignorance becomes knowledge. That was what the Messenger ﷺ and his Companions did, just as the messengers and their companions before them. And it is the lesson they left us to learn from.

Truth and benefaction were the essence of the role of the Messenger and his Companions. A pure and brave faith was their core principle. Because of those values, they bequeathed the best inheritance to humanity. They filled the human conscience with a sense of integrity.

Today, most radio stations worldwide openly broadcast verses from the glorious Quran. The Quran was a guide and a light to the Messenger ﷺ and his Companions. Now, all over the earth, in communities of Muslims, Christians, Jews, Hindus, Buddhists, atheists and so on - lofty minarets are erected to repeat the same words of the Messenger's muezzin 1400 years ago…

Allah is the Greatest, Allah is the Greatest
I bear witness that there is no god but Allah
I bear witness that Muhammad is the Messenger of Allah
Come to the Prayer
Come to success

The Quran is recited the world over; everywhere on earth the mosques are filled; and everywhere on earth its principles are celebrated. This all-pervading power comes only from belief in Allah, in the Messenger, and in all other messengers who came before. They truly gave everything to their cause and took nothing for themselves.

There remains one question raised by this study of the Prophet's Companions. The question is, "How could dispute have ruined the strong ties between the rightly guided brothers? And, how did the civil war (that broke out between Ali's supporters and those of Muawiyah) overpower this splendid brotherhood?"

In order to give an answer to this question, we have to go back to the virtue of faith in these Companions, and consider other historical factors as well. Indeed, their true, clear, and decisive faith had made them follow the same path. To them, truth had but one face which they recognised and followed. While the Messenger ﷺ was living among them, guidance to what is true and right - a matter in which people differed - was an easy matter. Revelation, or the Messenger (or a combination both), usually clarified every obscure or unintelligible matter.

When the Messenger ﷺ passed away, they never differed in what had been explained by Allah's revelation or through Muhammad's interpretation. However, when Uthman (may Allah be pleased with him) was killed, his murder was preceded and accompanied by a pernicious commotion that shook all Islamic nations at that time. As a consequence of that terrible occurrence, the dispute widened. It was inevitable for each Companion to choose to adopt one of the multiple views, according to his own demeanour.

Their way of choosing, like their way of believing, was characterised by clarity and decisiveness. There was no hesitation or hypocrisy. Those who were convinced of Imam Ali's point of view chose his side, and those convinced of Muawiyah's point of view chose his side. Some chose to be neutral and abandoned the dispute altogether.

The above concerns the Companions, the early believers in Islam who lived at the time of the Messenger ﷺ and fought with him the forces of polytheism and darkness. However, these Companions alone were not the 'centre of gravity' in the Islamic state at the time of the dispute between Ali and Muawiyah. This is because the state at that time had expanded tremendously, and a new power emerged and started to take part in and direct events. The best evidence for this is that the conspiracy to claim the life of Caliph Uthman and the agents assigned to carry it out came from outside Medina, rather from outside the Arab Peninsula. They came from some distant Islamic countries. Therefore, this new foreign power played a role which the first Companions struggled to repel.

This new power was effective in turning the dispute between Ali and Muawiyah into outright warfare. It was only then that the people of Syria sided with Muawiyah, and the people of Iraq sided with Ali, making them the real protagonists in that war. Even in the final analysis, the war was not between two Islamic camps as much as it was between two regional ones: the Syrians on one side and Iraqis on the other.

There was a third force which cannot be ignored, a force which lay in wait for Islam since it had its sovereignty demolished. That was the remnants of power in Persia and some few who continued to perpetuate their schemes against Islam through their many agents who infiltrated Islam by pretending to embrace it. Some of them were able to cause a lot of damage and destruction within the ranks of Muslims, which the defeated empires could not otherwise do alone.

We should also not ignore another fact, which is that each of the leaders never expected that the matter would develop to such a terrible degree. Imam Ali and his followers saw their advance towards Syria as merely a scare tactic. They genuinely thought that Muawiyah would soon realise the power of the state, and would respect and obey it.

On the other hand, Muawiyah and his followers believed that Imam Ali was merely testing their strength and their readiness. If he found them strong and well equipped, he would seek reconciliation through other means. Yet, the matter developed in a strange and unusual way. That sudden development points to the hidden forces who were at work in each camp to turn the dispute into full scale warfare.

Let us now conclude our discussion about this incident. As you may recall, Az-Zubair (may Allah be pleased with him) was fighting in the ranks of Muawiyah, but at the end of the battle he realised his mistake in joining the war altogether, and so he withdrew. However, some fighters followed him and stabbed him to death while he was praying. The killer amongst them robbed Az-Zubair of his sword and ran to Imam Ali, desiring to tell him the good news of the murder of Az-Zubair and to lay in his hands the sword he had used in fighting for Muawiyah against Ali. He came to the Imam's door asking for permission to enter. When Ali learned of the matter he shouted his command to dismiss the killer, saying, "Give the good tidings to the killer of Ibn Sufiyah that he will be cast in hellfire." By Ibn Sufiyah, he meant Az-Zubair (may Allah be pleased with him). He ordered further to have Az-Zubair's sword taken from the killer and brought to him.

When Ali saw the sword, he kept kissing it. He was crying and saying, "A sword whose owner had so many times removed the distress from the Messenger of Allah."

This remarkable scene bestows a strange kind tranquillity upon the painful disagreement between Ali and Muawiyah. It fills us with much understanding and appreciation of the Companions as they truly were when we remember it.

Now, we bid farewell to those men with whom we have travelled in the pages of this book. We thank Allah for His blessings, hoping to have more blessing, compassion, and good health from the Almighty.

With awe and reverence, we say to our eminent teacher, the last of the Messengers, "May the peace and mercy of Allah and His blessings be upon you. May Allah grant you the best reward for the teachings you gave and for your guidance." And with a renewed appreciation, we say to his blessed Companions, "Peace, Righteous Companions". It is a peace we extended at the start of this journey with awe and reverence; and it is a peace that remains in that awe and reverence, as we draw to a close.

www.ingramcontent.com/pod-product-compliance
Lightning Source LLC
Chambersburg PA
CBHW011316080526
44588CB00020B/2726

* 9 7 8 1 9 1 5 5 7 0 0 7 9 *